England's Unlikely Commander:

The Military Career of Æthelred the Unready

B r a n d o n   M .   B e n d e r

CONTENTS

ACKNOWLEDGMENTS

This short book could not have been written without the assistance of several helpful and knowledgeable people. I offer my sincerest thanks to: Dr. William Stockton, who in 2017 encouraged me to submit a proposal on this topic to The Kansas Association of Historians. That presentation spiraled out of control and, after many revisions and expansions, became this manuscript; to Dr. Eleanor Parker, who provided valuable and insightful feedback on an early version of this project. I owe her thanks for not only encouraging me to continue my research, but on a more specific level, for pointing me toward the Ælfrician manuscript addressed in Chapter Four and for helping me navigate the nuances of using later sagas and traditions (like the one in Chapter Five), or parts of them, as historical sources; to Dr. Simon J. Cook of *Rounded Globe*, who provided me a place to publish my research and also doubled as a sharp proofreader and editor; to *Rounded Globe*'s Drew Holgate, who was instrumental to setting up the online version of this manuscript; to Brenda A. Brown, who provided feedback on readability, wording, and content throughout the writing process; to the peer reviewer who provided expert advice and feedback on my scholarship, often catching details and inconsistencies (and bringing up new ideas) that I had not even thought of.

Only later did I find out that this peer reviewer was none other than Dr. Levi Roach, a leading expert on Æthelred's reign whose own research plays a leading role in this book. His direct contribution to this manuscript (along with his existing scholarship) was invaluable; to my friends, family, and coworkers, who have been enthusiastic and unwavering in their support; and finally, to Ellen Brewer, who provided encouragement and constructive criticism on virtually every aspect of this book. My sincerest thanks to all of you.

INTRODUCTION

Perhaps no English monarch has suffered a poorer reputation than Æthelred the Unready, especially militarily. In many respects, his reputation is unsurprising. Under Æthelred (reigned 978-1013, 1014-16), England was devastated by recurring Viking invasions. The kingdom was even briefly toppled by and subjected to a Danish king, only for Æthelred to return to the throne a few months later. England would fall to a Danish ruler a second time after Æthelred's death, making the reign look like a complete disaster in hindsight. Accordingly, one of the most common — and damning — allegations against Æthelred is that he was militarily inactive and ineffective. Undoubtedly, military success goes a long way in aiding the reputation of a medieval monarch. Revered English kings, such as Alfred, are strongly associated with their triumphs on the battlefield. Even stereotypically tyrannical monarchs, like William the Conqueror, earn begrudging respect for their military prowess, if nothing else. The opposite is also true, especially in Æthelred's case; for centuries, writers have complained of Æthelred's supposed idleness in the face of danger, chastising him for not being more active in facing down the Viking threat.[1]

Even early on, Æthelred's military reputation was mediocre at best. For example, the main source for Æthelred's reign, the *Anglo-Saxon Chronicle*, paints a gloomy picture of the era.[2] Written just after Æthelred's death and the fall of Anglo-Saxon England, the *Chronicle* speaks of lavish payments to the Vikings, treacherous military leaders, and entire seasons where the Saxon army marched all over the country without forcing the Vikings out. By the 1100s, the king's military reputation — and his reputation in general — was in freefall. The eminent medieval historian William of Malmesbury famously called the king's reign "disgraceful in its ending" (among many other harsh words), almost certainly with the Danish Conquest in mind.[3] The king also earned his infamous nickname, *Unraed*, around this time, which means "badly-counselled" (*Unraed* is a pun on the name Æthelred, which actually means "noble-counsel"). As the language evolved, the name became distorted into "Unready," which we still call him today, only adding to the perception of a sluggish and inactive monarch.

Centuries later, Æthelred's military legacy remains poor, even in popular culture. In fact, the king's military reputation may have reached its nadir not in a peer-reviewed article, but in a play. In 1968, Æthelred was featured as the main character in Ronald Ribman's *The Ceremony of Innocence*, which portrayed him as a pacifist who would do anything to avoid fighting the Vikings.[4] Holed up in a monastery, Ribman's Æthelred would much rather pray and rail against the futility and senselessness of war than command an army. Although *Ceremony* takes numerous historical liberties, it is still notable that Ribman chose Æthelred as his mouthpiece for pacifism and military avoidance. When in need of an absentee commander, Æthelred was apparently the man to call on.

Modern historians have likewise criticized the king's military abilities, pointing out that Æthelred sometimes neglected to lead his armies in person and that he often organized massive payments of silver (known as "tribute") to secure temporary peace for his country. Even those who acknowledge that the king did ride into battle almost dismiss his efforts out of hand. For instance, one popular historian correctly notes that Æthelred personally led a damaging attack on Strathclyde and the Isle of Man in 1000, but just as soon downplays it, suggesting that the king was "vent[ing] his frustration on the hapless landscape."[5] Although the writer goes on to suggest more realistic motives for the attack, this quote is the very first explanation offered. The king's reputation clearly precedes him, obscuring the underlying rationale behind such raids and expeditions.

In recent decades, however, some scholars have adopted a more nuanced view of Æthelred's military abilities, conceding that he was more proactive than previously thought. In 1970, Frank Barlow recognized Æthelred's efforts, calling him "a most active prince, a vigorous soldier, fertile in schemes for victory, always experimenting, always trying, [and] never giving up hope."[6] However, this quote comes from a biography of Æthelred's son, Edward the Confessor, and Barlow says little more about the father's military abilities. In the early 1980s, BBC presenter Michael Wood also gave Æthelred some much-needed credit, frequently making note of the king's military actions, although never in-depth since his documentary focused on the wider reign.[7] Æthelred's full-length biographies by Ryan Lavelle, Ann Williams, Levi Roach, and Richard Abels likewise recognize the king's surprisingly forceful nature, although like Wood, their focus is on the reign as a whole.[8] Perhaps the closest look at the king's military ventures comes from Ian Howard, who wrote on Sweyn Forkbeard's Viking invasions of England (and by extension, some of Æthelred's campaigns).[9] That said, the numerous and surprising military campaigns of Æthelred the Unready have yet to be the sole focus of an in-depth publication.

The military actions of Æthelred, while they cannot be separated from the wider reign, are worthy of attention in their own right. Æthelred did not sit passively while the Vikings took his kingdom. As it turns out, despite their individual biases, sources like the *Chronicle*, the *Gesta Normannorum Ducum*, the *Textus Roffensis*, and even the *Saga of Olaf Haraldsson* portray the king as far more militarily active than he is normally given credit for. Using these sources, it becomes clear King Æthelred was militarily engaged throughout his long reign and frequently used force to achieve his aims. He organized his armies, constructed navies, defended his cities, re-fortified his strongholds, aggressively attacked his neighbors, and became one of the few English kings to ever reconquer his kingdom after being deposed.

A Note on Names and Sources

Because this work deals with historical figures whose names may be archaic or unfamiliar, there are many ways to render these names into Modern English. I have tried to conform to the most common practices for each name. Archaic names are usually compromises between their original spellings and Modern English conventions — for example, Æthelred instead of Æþelraed — which I have echoed in this book. Alternate spellings like Aethelred and Ethelred are also common, so I have left naming variations alone when they appear in quotes. Names that have survived into modern times, like Alfred and Edward, are given their modern spellings even if they looked different in Old English (Ælfred and Eadweard). And finally, I have decided to anglicize foreign names for readability purposes (thus Canute and Olaf instead of Knutr and Olafr).

Another challenge that comes with writing about a period so distant is the scarcity and reliability of sources. Obviously, writing about Anglo-Saxon England is not like writing a biography of John F. Kennedy or a book on World War II. Whereas those fields are blessed with plenty of detailed, primary sources like journals and interviews, early medieval sources are few and far between — sometimes written decades after the events they describe and with obvious biases, contradictions, or factual errors. Some of them, like the *Chronicle*, can be quite terse. Thankfully, there are far more sources for Æthelred's reign than for earlier eras of English history, like the 5th or 6th centuries. In a way, I am lucky to have as much to work with as I do. That said, at times throughout this work, it is necessary to stop and consider where our information has come from and to analyze what it could mean — and how useful or trustworthy it is. While I have not tried to be overly-conservative or unduly cautious, it simply comes with the territory.

CHAPTER ONE

THE EARLY YEARS (978-990)

Æthelred became King of the English in 978, during what we would today call his preteen years.[10] He inherited a kingdom that had not seen serious armed confrontation in decades, when King Eadred fought to expel Eric Bloodaxe from Northumbria in the 940s and 950s.[11] The reign of Æthelred's father, Edgar (959-975), was so notable for its lack of armed conflict that it became attached to the king's very name: Edgar the Peaceful.[12] After Edgar's death in 975, the reign of his eldest son Edward lasted three more years, again devoid of recorded military action.

However, Edgar's tranquil reign proved to be the exception rather than the rule in the wider history of Anglo-Saxon England, and this broader context will be helpful to fully understand Æthelred's later actions. Although it is tempting to think of early England as one indivisible kingdom, in part because its rulers had already adopted the title *King of the English*, the nation still had serious cracks and divisions beneath the surface. The rival petty kingdoms that made up early England had only been consolidated under the House of Wessex since the 920s and 930s, and even then with difficulty. In 957, rival factions had divided the kingdom between King Eadwig (955-959) and his younger brother, Edgar. Although this division is easy to overlook as an anomaly (especially since Edgar succeeded to the whole country just two years later), it shows that powerful factions could still fragment the nominally unified kingdom. Factionalism also affected Æthelred's early life: King Edgar had sponsored widespread monastic reform throughout his reign, building resentment among the secular clergy as well as nobles who had lost land to the church. When Edgar died, these rivalries seem to have become even more intense.

Edgar's death in 975 also unleashed a volatile succession dispute between backers of his eldest son, Edward, and the younger (but arguably more "legitimate") Æthelred.[13] The Anglo-Saxons did not have formal succession laws; instead, claimants were "elected" by a loose group of nobles and clergymen called the *witan*. The *witan* eventually settled on Edward, but tensions between the groups lived on — the assassination of King Edward just three years later was carried out by members of Æthelred's own party, paving the way for Æthelred to begin his long but troubled reign.

Few modern historians seriously consider that Æthelred played a role in his brother's killing; he was no more than 12 at the time. Likewise, he could do little to address the country's religious disputes. More importantly,

Æthelred's accession helps illustrate the precarious situation that he inherited: a nation that had been free of Viking conflict — and indeed, armed conflict in general — since the 940s and 950s, yet one that was also at the mercy of regional, political, and even religious factions.

An informal regency council oversaw Æthelred's first few years on the throne, led by his mother, Queen Ælfthryth, and Bishop Æthelwold of Winchester. In 984, though, Bishop Æthelwold died and the teenage Æthelred appears to have broken free, suddenly spurning the influence of his mother and exercising his newfound authority. Although the *Chronicle* says that isolated Viking raids had resumed by this point, they were probably not yet seen as a national threat.[14] Fittingly, Æthelred's first hint of military action took place during these years, and not against Vikings armies. Instead, just as his majority rule began, the king used force to assert his authority over his own subjects.

The Razing of Rochester (986 AD)

Newly independent, Æthelred made his first display of military force in 986, attacking the Diocese of Rochester. While the *Chronicle* records the event, it devotes just two words to the attack itself, saying that "the king *laid waste* to the diocese of Rochester" (emphasis mine).[15] This is a catch-all term used by the *Chronicle* for complete military destruction, consisting of anything from looting and burning to widespread slaughter. If the severity of this attack is still in doubt, the *Chronicle* uses the same term for William the Conqueror's infamous campaigns in 1069-70, better known as the Harrying of the North.

That said, there are plenty of more detailed references to this attack, making it (despite the brevity of the *Chronicle*) one of the best-attested military actions of King Æthelred. A firsthand account of this incident can be found in the king's own charters, where he takes full responsibility for the command. "In the time of my youth, I dragged [this land] away from the diocese of the church of Rochester," Æthelred says in a charter from 998 restoring some of this property to the church. "In fact, its despoilment by plunder I ordered to take place."[16] This is far and away our most direct account of the conflict, written in the king's own voice. Regardless of whether Æthelred wrote or dictated the charter himself, the surprisingly repentant tone suggests the king must have been closely involved in its production and message. "Now, in the presence of God, with tearful contrition of heart, I repent it all," he says. "Every advantage pertaining to that same place I freely restore, hoping my tears of penance will be received." The king blames the attack on the influence of his advisors, but Æthelred may not be giving us the full story — he appears more concerned with piety and reconciliation, so he has not left us the full political context here.

Later accounts by Osbern of Canterbury and Sulcard of Westminster give further details, explaining that the king had granted land in Rochester to one of his followers, but that Bishop Ælfstan expelled this follower, provoking Æthelred.[17] According to Osbern, Æthelred continued to devastate Rochester until Dunstan, the aged Archbishop of Canterbury, bribed him to stop with 100 pounds of silver.[18] In any case, church lands were not off limits to the young king — an important distinction to make after the religious and monastic reform of his father's reign.[19] In fact, only when considering the monastic and anti-monastic factions that emerged under Edgar does the Rochester attack fully make sense. In the wake of Edgar's reforms, many nobles lost land to religious houses, and as Ann Williams notes, they had every right to be concerned about their own positions.[20] When Æthelred came of age and aligned himself with some of these nobles, he granted them land and power at the expense of the church. The king was breaking with the status quo and steering the country in a different direction. Even though the accounts of Sulcard and Osbern add more detail, there is no reason to believe they are especially embellished or exaggerated accounts — while they are more dramatic, they do fit squarely with the political realities and factions of the time.

So, if the king was breaking with his father's policies, and he had granted land to a favorite who was refused access to this land, the attack becomes not so much sacrilegious as it does a political move. Refusing to acknowledge the king's land grant (intentionally or mistakenly) was a direct challenge to the authority of King Æthelred. As even the *Chronicle's* terse account makes clear, regardless of what sparked the conflict, the young monarch's response was swift and fierce, flying in the face of his traditional reputation. Even if Æthelred was not actively looking for an excuse to lash out, he clearly jumped at the opportunity: he was young, unproven, and had only recently gained full control of the government. Although the attack was politically provocative, and although Æthelred was later repentant, destroying Rochester was a success for the young king. Bishop Ælfstan was alienated from court, disappearing from witness lists during the late 980s.[21] Æthelred had gotten his way, and had used brute force to achieve it.

CHAPTER TWO

DEFENSE AND DIPLOMACY (991-999)

Meanwhile, Viking activity had resumed shortly after Æthelred wasted Rochester in 986. Again, these initial Viking attacks seem to have been minor, isolated raids rather than part of any formal, large-scale invasion. They are not presented as dire until 991, when the English fought the Battle of Maldon, later immortalized in one of the nation's great poems.[22] Vikings under Olaf Tryggvason landed near the town of Maldon and defeated Byrhtnoth, the ealdorman (or regional leader) who organized the English response.[23] *The Battle of Maldon* poem presents the battle as long and fierce, with the English putting up a stout defense. Moreover, the English themselves are presented as united and eager to fight, hailing from all over the kingdom.

How literally the historian should interpret this "united" image will probably always be up for debate. That said, the poem is by far our most detailed account of the battle (the *Chronicle* likewise mentions this battle and its basic details), giving us good reason to believe that even at a local level, the kingdom's defenses were not in shambles under King Æthelred; despite decades of relative inactivity, and despite the successful "pirate raids" in the 980s, the English did not shy away from pitched battle against a large Norse army — 93 ships strong, according to the *Chronicle*.

The First Fleet (992)

The king himself was not present at Maldon, nor was he expected to be; Viking fleets often appeared and vanished faster than royal armies could assemble. His response, though, shows him to be a ruler aware of military realities, not an out-of-touch, do-nothing king. In the wake of the battle, Æthelred paid a tribute of 10,000 pounds to Olaf and then ordered a massive fleet to organize the following year. The king decreed that "all ships that were of any use should be collected at London," and the assembled ships should then "entrap the host somewhere out to sea."[24] While the king's tribute payment is frequently criticized, his command for a fleet the very next year is often overlooked.

Unfortunately for the king, treachery ruined his fleet. One of the men he had selected to command it, Ealdorman Ælfric of Hampshire, warned the enemy before the English could attack. The *Chronicle* does say that the English fleet engaged Viking raiders later on, but the emphasis is clearly on the treachery of Ælfric.[25] Nonetheless, the organization of the English fleet showed that Æthelred was capable of foresight and decisiveness. In addition, the king had strategically used tribute to buy time and orchestrate a national response after the defeat at Maldon, not as a solution in its own right. This behavior was not unique at the time. English and Frankish kings had frequently paid tributes to Viking invaders throughout the 9th and 10th centuries; even Æthelred's great-great grandfather, Alfred the Great, had utilized tribute. Despite anachronistic comparisons to Neville Chamberlain appeasing Hitler, in Æthelred's own time the payment of such tribute was neither scandalous nor uncommon; it was even used by militaristic rulers like William the Conqueror, who paid Sweyn II of Denmark to leave the country in 1069. In reality, tributes were a proven way to stop immediate damage and organize a more effective military response.

The Great Levies and the Blinding of Ælfgar (993)

Another brief account of English resistance appears in 993, when the *Chronicle* notes that "great levies" (or "great armies")[26] were assembled to fight a Viking host who had destroyed Bamburgh.[27] We are not told who ordered the army to assemble, but the use of the word "great" seems to imply something larger than Byrhtnoth's force from 991. The most likely candidate is Æthelred himself; in a realm still divided by regional differences, the king was often the only person capable of uniting the various factions and families. However, just as with the fleet from

992, this assembly fell apart. Again, the *Chronicle* spares the king of any blame, naming three commanders who "were the first to set the example of flight." Just as before, our best source for this era paints the king's response as rational but blames military failures on the next rung of leadership. This is notable because the *Chronicle* was written after Æthelred's death and his kingdom's collapse, when it would have been advantageous for a scribe writing in the reign of Canute to blame Æthelred for failures, or at least to avoid showing any affection for him. And yet many of the worst military aspects of the entire reign, as further chapters will discuss, are ascribed to local leaders, while the king's actions are noted as successful. This was even present in the Rochester account, a military show of force simply attributed to "the king."

Æthelred also took brutal action against one of his former favorites, Ælfgar, in 993, blinding him.[28] Shocking as it may seem in modern times, the blinding of a court figure would not be so notable if this Ælfgar were not the son of Ælfric — the ealdorman who had betrayed the king a year prior. The *Chronicle*, unfortunately, gives no clues about what (if any) role Ælfgar played in his father's betrayal and defection, although Ælfgar may have been punished for despoiling church lands.[29] This means that Ælfgar's punishment cannot be viewed in isolation as a reaction to military affairs alone, and that there may have been several reasons for his fall from power.

In any case, after Ælfric's military treachery, he and his son were out of favor with the king. Ælfgar's mutilation shows that Æthelred would not tolerate those who fell short of his military and moral expectations. Notably, the *Chronicle* places this detail immediately after the "great levies" incident that same year, when the three commanders had fled. An intriguing possibility emerges when the account is read this way: in blinding Ælfgar, Æthelred was not just sending a warning to those associated with the traitor Ælfric, but to all who showed reluctance, deceit, or cowardice on the battlefield.

The Siege of London and Truce with Olaf (994)

The next year, the kingdom faced another challenge when Olaf Tryggvason returned. With a similarly-sized fleet of 94 ships, Olaf boldly sailed up the Thames and unleashed an "unceasing attack" on London, even setting it on fire.[30] However, the Londoners resisted fiercely, causing Olaf and his army to flee to the countryside, where they could do more damage. Finally, after much destruction, "the king and his councillors" offered Olaf 16,000 pounds worth of tribute to cease his destruction. This episode also has some parallels to Maldon. First, the kingdom's defenses, especially near fortified towns like Maldon and London, proved capable. Even though the Londoners were successful and the English at Maldon were not, both seem to have inflicted serious damage on Olaf's forces. Second, the king again offered tribute only after military efforts had failed, not as a solution in its own right. The next year, Æthelred sought a diplomatic solution to Olaf's raiding, turning the Viking leader into a friendly Christian ally.[31] The *Chronicle* reports Æthelred stood as Olaf's sponsor in a "great ceremony" for Olaf's Christian confirmation, offering him lavish gifts. In return, Olaf promised never to attack the English again — a promise he kept. In addition, many of these Vikings then switched sides, entering Æthelred's pay and agreeing to defend the coasts from other Viking bands.[32] This is another sign that the king's tribute payments were not merely "protection money," but could be used as contracts to secure mercenaries — it was a hefty price, but for a very valuable service.

As for Olaf, not only had Æthelred given him wealth, but he had also provided him with a sense of legitimacy and prestige; Olaf was now a confirmed Christian, with a powerful and wealthy European monarch as his sponsor. Olaf would spend the rest of his life fighting a bloodthirsty war of conversion and conquest in Scandinavia, tying up other Viking bands that may otherwise have been free to attack England. In 995 and 996, there are no attacks recorded in England, implying that the king's new defenders were capable deterrents.

The Raids Resume (997-998)

But Olaf and his rivals were not the only Norse leaders with their sights set on England, and more attacks are recorded in 997 and 998, with widespread destruction recorded in Wales, Devon, and Cornwall.[33] The *Chronicle* is limited in its description of the English response for these years, colored with notable pessimism and blanket statements. It notes that many armies were assembled, but that the Vikings "always… had the victory" and that the English leaders constantly gave orders to retreat. However, there are some reasons to suspect that despite these obvious failures, the situation was not nearly as dire as we are led to believe. While the chronicler seems to describe a nation in crisis, other evidence from this time suggests that, in most places, life continued as usual.[34]

The first bit of evidence comes from a pair of noticeable omissions in the *Chronicle* — the king himself is not mentioned with these armies, nor does he order any more tributes. While it is possible that this is an oversight by the chronicler, he does mention the king in connection with military events from 986, 992, 993, 994, and frequently again from 999 and after. While a more traditional view might highlight these omissions as proof of Æthelred's lack of military involvement (a view proven wrong by his presence in other campaigns), another possibility is that these raids were best dealt with by local leaders, and that a tribute was not necessary. The *Chronicle* seems to imply that the "host" of 997-98 was one band that traveled along the southern coast, leaving the majority of the kingdom unaffected.

Historians have also seized on the wording of the *Chronicle* for 997, which says the raiders pillaged inland "until they came to Lydford," speculating that the Vikings were actually stopped at this point because Lydford was heavily fortified.[35] Although the Vikings continued their looting later, the possibility that the raiders were repelled at Lydford is worth noting. It also falls in line with previous events where Vikings faced stiff opposition around the king's *burhs* (or fortified towns). The *burh* system dated back to the reign of Alfred (871-899), who used it to protect his people against the "Great Heathen Army." As seen with Maldon and London, these fortifications were clearly not in disrepair under Æthelred and continued to function as effective strongholds. In regard to Lydford in particular, the *Chronicle's* wording is ambiguous enough that we can never be certain why the Vikings turned around. The earthworks and fortifications at Lydford almost certainly would have factored into the Vikings' decision, though, regardless of whether an actual battle or siege took place.

Another sign of stability comes from the state of art, literature, and coinage, which flourished during King Æthelred's reign, especially in these early decades. Not only does *The Battle of Maldon* poem come from these years, but our earliest copy of *Beowulf* has also been dated to Æthelred's reign, with the year 1000 as a baseline. Robert Lacey and Danny Danziger likewise recognize that England may actually have been in a strong state during this era. In their book *The Year 1000*, they heap praise on Æthelred and his government, something almost unheard of among popular historians, who often provide a caricature of a hapless king instead. Lacey and Danziger note that "if Ethelred Unraed... had died in or around the year 1000, he might have a reputation to match that of his distinguished forebear Athelstan," the first king to fully unite England.[36]

While a comparison to Æthelstan may seem like an overstatement, this sentiment is echoed in formal academic circles, too. Ian Howard, for example, is highly skeptical of the bleak picture painted by the chronicler from 997-99.[37] The English government was probably not in the dire straits that the chronicler recalls, and it was certainly not without redeeming qualities. The Vikings left a trail of destruction across the southern coast, but the nation was not on the verge of collapse. Æthelred himself even seemed preoccupied with other matters near the end of the 10th century, spending much of his time writing new law codes. Abels goes so far as to call Æthelred a "prolific legislator" and points out that much of that legislation dates from the 990s.[38] So despite the southern raids, Æthelred does seem to have "brought England's first millennium to a laudable close" by using a careful balance of defense and diplomacy.[39] Things did not always go as planned, but Æthelred's kingdom persisted nonetheless.

Calling out the Army and Navy (999)

In 999, however, the king turned his attention back to military affairs. Vikings had faced off against local forces in Kent in "a sharp encounter," where even our dismissive chronicler concedes that the English fought well. But with Kentish levies defeated, Æthelred immediately called out a national army, commanding that his men should confront the invaders on both land and sea. However, the naval fleet seems to have been poorly managed and plagued by delays, inefficiency, and irresolution. "The more urgent a thing was, the greater was the delay from one hour to the next," the *Chronicle* complains, calling the English expeditions "a complete failure" and describing how Vikings chased the English far inland. The events of 999 have been held up frequently as an example of Æthelred's alleged military incompetence, but the entry for 1000 says that the Vikings left for Normandy. Did the invaders vanish on their own accord or did Æthelred's forces actually accomplish some of their goals?[40] While it is impossible to know for sure, the more important point to remember for Æthelred's reputation is that he advocated for war in 999, not peace, even with the rest of the country doing relatively well.

CHAPTER THREE

A BURST OF ENERGY
(1000-1002)

Around the year 1000, we see a very different Æthelred.
The king, by then in his early 30s, frequently and directly
involved himself in the fighting.[41] The *Chronicle* does
not explicitly suggest reasons for this sudden change in
strategy, but there are several possibilities to consider. The
first and most obvious is that the intensity of Viking raids
themselves had increased since the 980s, putting Æthelred
under more pressure to act. As noted in the previous
chapter, England clearly had other priorities for much of
the 980s and 990s, as evidenced by the king's law codes
and the output of art and literature. Perhaps by 1000,
it was becoming clear that the Vikings were no longer a
nuisance to be dealt with locally but should be confronted
directly by the king.

A more intriguing possibility has to do with
Æthelred's long-term dynastic ambitions. As a former

boy-king, Æthelred knew firsthand how important it was to have a mature ruler at the helm. Æthelred married young and had many children, but during the 980s and 990s, even the eldest would have been too young to rule. So, as Lavelle notes, should Æthelred have died in battle during these years, he had no adult sons and no brothers left to assume the throne. Although Æthelred did lead and gather forces during the 980s and 990s, this could partially explain why around 1000, with his eldest sons well into their teens, the king's activity became far more aggressive.

Whatever the reason, around the new millennium, Æthelred led armies into foreign lands and concocted ambitious plans to solve the Viking problem. Even the coinage from this period, as Wood notes, "shows the helmeted Æthelred in a militant mood, armed and vigilant, ready to protect his flock."[42] The king began acting aggressively toward both his neighbors and his own citizens from 1000-02.

Attacking Strathclyde and the Isle of Man (1000)

In 1000, the *Chronicle* records that Æthelred launched an attack by land and sea against the Kingdom of Strathclyde and the Isle of Man, two semi-independent realms that may have been allied by this period.[43] While Frank Stenton calls the motive for these expeditions "part of the lost history of the north," it is feasible to work out Æthelred's intentions.[44] The most likely interpretation is that Æthelred sought to punish these regions for their Norse cooperation, a view shared by other medieval historians.[45] "The English king Æthelred opened the eleventh century by leading an army into Cumberlande [Strathclyde] and attacking the Isle of Man," says Fiona Edmonds, noting that "the manoeuvre followed a build-up of Scandinavian activity" in the area.[46] Both areas assisted in raids on England at this time, either as recruiting pools, places to unload stolen treasure, or launching points for future attacks.

With England free from raids in 1000, Æthelred personally led his army north to Strathclyde, with devastating effects, "laying waste to most of the country."[47] A naval fleet, perhaps some of the same ships from 992 and 999, planned to rendezvous with the king as well, but for whatever reason it "failed to contact him" and instead ravaged the Isle of Man.[48] Either way, Æthelred's attack on Strathclyde was a success. He was not simply taking his anger out on bystanders; he was retaliating against his enemies, expanding his influence beyond traditional English borders, and proving himself willing to engage in violence. Even the ravaging of the Isle of Man, though Æthelred was not able to meet his fleet, must have accomplished some of the king's goals. His soldiers had occupied the Isle of Man, a region known for Norse cooperation, and devastated it by their presence while he personally oversaw the destruction of Strathclyde, its nearby ally.

It is also worth noting that besides the punitive undertones, some historians have interpreted the Strathclyde and Isle of Man attacks as imperial expeditions. For instance, Lavelle mentions that in a charter from shortly after these raids, Æthelred calls himself the "king of the whole island," offering a glimpse into his mindset at the time.[49] Howard compares the attacks to Æthelstan's wars of expansion (another comparison to England's illustrious first king), noting that Æthelred came from a long line of conquerors.[50] In addition, while Strathclyde did have its own rulers at the time, its leadership would collapse by the end of Æthelred's reign. In the interlude, it is likely that these leaders would have acknowledged Æthelred as an overlord. It is impossible to tell what long-term impact, if any, the English attacks had on the decline of Strathclyde, but the sources of this period are clear: King Æthelred had made his presence known in the northwest in 1000.

The Invasion of Normandy (1000-02)

Around the same time,[51] William of Jumieges — a Norman writing around the 1070s — says that Æthelred crossed the channel and attacked Normandy. This is interesting considering that the *Chronicle* places the Vikings there in 1000. With the attacks on Strathclyde, the Isle of Man, and Normandy, a clear pattern emerges: the king was punishing those who had funded or sheltered his enemies. The Normans, Viking descendants themselves, clearly sympathized with their Norse relatives, and this had caused problems between the Normans and English before. In 991, Pope John XV even intervened to help negotiate a treaty between Æthelred and Duke Richard I of Normandy, where the two rulers agreed to stop aiding each other's enemies.[52] Duke Richard II, who ascended in 996, does not appear to have upheld his father's end of the bargain. Æthelred may have perceived Richard II as not only a danger to England, but an oath-breaker. William of

Jumieges records in the *Gesta Normannorum Ducum* that Æthelred personally led an invasion of Normandy, seeking to capture Richard.[53] The attack failed, repelled by a local count named Nigel. William says that Æthelred's men were badly defeated by Nigel and local peasants, including women. Æthelred blushed with embarrassment when he realized how poorly his attack had gone, according to William. Regardless of how much truth lies in the flamboyant details, like the kidnapping plot, fighting maidens, and a blushing Æthelred, the English invasion of Normandy still shows the king quite differently than how popular culture portrays him.[54] Rather than a battle-shy monarch, the real Æthelred was unafraid of pressuring foreign neighbors with violence and leading a cross-channel invasion himself, especially if it meant punishing known allies of Viking raiders.

The aftermath saw Æthelred marry Emma of Normandy, Richard's sister, in 1002.[55] Perhaps a marriage alliance was Æthelred's attempt to buy peace after force had failed. That said, Æthelred's invasion must have pressured the duke, as well. Would Æthelred attack again if not pacified? Making peace with the king was far more beneficial, especially given his sudden increase in activity. The resulting marriage alliance was designed to please both sides. Richard would not aid Æthelred's Viking enemies, and Æthelred would not raid Richard's territory.

"Courageous Resistance" and the Betrayal of Pallig (1001)

While Æthelred himself had been going on the offensive since the turn of the millennium, more clues about the state of the home defenses come in 1001. In that year, Viking hordes returned to England after their brief absence in 1000. Two accounts in the *Chronicle* tell of how the English fought back: one says that after the Vikings penetrated far inland, they were met by English soldiers in Hampshire, where 81 Englishmen were slain, including some of the king's own officials (or "reeves"). Notably, the annalist again hints that the English fought well, saying that losses "on the Danish side were heavier, but they had possession of the place of slaughter." This represents a rare departure from the image of the king's leaders fleeing from battle. Instead, despite in all likelihood being outnumbered, they gave their lives to defend their land and inflicted great damage on their enemy.

In the same year, a Norse army besieged a fortress along the River Exe but was repelled by what the *Chronicle* calls "a solid and courageous resistance." Then, as they often did after a defeat, the Vikings fled to the open countryside where they could ravage and loot unhindered. Just like with Maldon in 991, London in 994, and possibly Lydford in 997, the king's system of *burhs* proved capable. As noted in the previous chapter, Æthelred refurbished these defenses continually throughout his reign and, from the words of the *Chronicle*, they were often too difficult for even the Vikings to topple — something Æthelred deserves credit for if he also shoulders some of the blame for failures.

The king's ego must have suffered a blow that same year, though, because he was betrayed by one of his regional leaders — a Norse mercenary and landowner named Pallig.

The *Chronicle* records that after the battle at Hampshire, Pallig defected from "the allegiance he owed King Æthelred," amassing men and ships to help the Viking army plunder the country. Pallig's background and origins are murky at best, but he seems to have been a Scandinavian chieftain who served Æthelred as a mercenary, perhaps recruited as part of the earlier peace agreements. The *Chronicle* records the treachery of Pallig with obvious disgust, commenting that he helped raid the country he was supposed to defend "contrary to all the pledges he had given Æthelred." The king had granted Pallig land and wealth, showing that he was willing to pay a fair price for the cooperation of a skilled mercenary. That said, the desertion of Pallig seems to have bolstered the Viking host of 1001, compounding a worsening situation for the English; the Norse raiders plundered the country at will until English forces caught them at Pinhoe. The Vikings were victorious in the battle, however, and subsequently destroyed countless manors across the country. The *Chronicle* insists that from this point on, resistance collapsed, with the raiders plundering and terrorizing the region as they pleased.

Tribute and the St. Brice's Day Massacre (1002)

Finally, King Æthelred orchestrated a tribute payment in 1002 to put an end to the chaos. Like before, this "protection money" had clearly not been the first solution: in 1001 alone, the English had defended their towns, been defeated at least twice, seen numerous royal officials killed, been betrayed by one of their protectors, and witnessed numerous estates destroyed before the king sued for peace. Although Æthelred is usually depicted as far too eager to throw money at the Vikings, an English subject in 1002 might have felt just the opposite way after all these defeats and hardships. Maybe it seemed as though the raiders could not be bought off soon enough, especially in the areas directly affected, a sentiment that the annalist would echo in the coming years.[56] But while tribute was a tried and true solution that Æthelred had used before, it may have seemed that the English were out of options. The king and his councilors had one last idea up their sleeves — one that was decidedly more desperate and sinister.

The final act of this "burst of energy" was the St. Brice's Day Massacre, when Æthelred ordered the systematic execution of all Danes in England. He commanded this, the *Chronicle* says, because the Vikings were plotting to assassinate him. This order was probably only carried out in areas where Scandinavians were minorities, as much of "the Danelaw" was heavily populated with Norse descendants. Nonetheless, the massacre was carried out in some parts of the country, which the king himself confirms in a later charter. As with Rochester, he readily admits his role in the act, but this time, there would be no repentance. Writing in 1004, Æthelred declares that the execution of England's Danes had been "a most just extermination."[57] The St. Brice's Day Massacre represents one of the most dramatic events of the entire reign, but exactly who it was meant to punish remains unclear.

For example, although popular culture often presents the massacre as flat-out genocide, scholars like Simon Keynes think that, given the events of 1001,

Viking mercenaries were actually the prime targets.[58] This would make the massacre, at least in part, a way of purging disloyal military leaders and making an example of traitors, similar to the blinding of Ælfgar in 993. St. Brice's Day may have started as an attempt to punish treacherous mercenaries and snowballed into a killing of Danes in general, or perhaps both were originally the intended targets. The *Chronicle* does not discriminate, as mentioned earlier, only saying that the order demanded the deaths of all Danes in England because Æthelred was told they would murder him. However, if we peer deeper into this description of royal paranoia, there may be more hints. With regards to the assassination plot, the annalist may be referring to Norse leaders here, not commoners. Commoners would not have been in a position to orchestrate the assassination of Æthelred and all of his advisors, who were also targets in this alleged plot. Moreover, while there were plenty of Norse settlers and descendants in England, most of them were farther north — there were significantly fewer of them in the south, where Æthelred was based. In fact, the king only ventured into the north and the Danelaw a handful of times in his entire 38-year reign.

Another clue that hints at military, rather than civilian, targets is a recently-unearthed mass grave in Ridgeway Hill. Archaeologists found over 50 beheaded bodies in a grave there that dated from around the year 1000. Almost immediately, researchers speculated that these burial pits were connected with St. Brice's Day. Not only do the Ridgeway Hill bodies date from around Æthelred's reign, but they appear to have been Norse warriors. "Aethelred was known for playing divide and conquer with bands of Scandinavian mercenaries who worked for him," says a news release from Cambridge. "It may be that these Vikings had fallen out of favour with the king."[59] It is tempting to suggest they are Æthelred's mercenaries from the early 1000s, systematically executed for disloyalty; but even if the bodies are not from the massacre, mercenaries would have fallen under this sweeping order by default. If we take the *Chronicle* at its word, commoner and mercenary alike would have been fair game. Æthelred was enforcing his military standards, albeit in an uncharacteristically dark way.[60]

The massacre was an appalling act, even by medieval standards, but as Roach writes, "we do not have to approve of Æthelred's actions in order to comprehend them."[61] St. Brice's Day and the tribute paid the same year obscure Æthelred's previous attempts to assert himself. Since 999, the king had called out his national army four times and launched two foreign invasions affecting three regions. At the same time, local warriors engaged or fended off the Vikings repeatedly. Even St. Brice's Day shows that Æthelred was anything but paralyzed at the turn of the millennium. The events of 1000-02 show a king who would use force to get his way, whether he used direct methods or underhanded ones.

CHAPTER FOUR

THE GROWING CRISIS (1003-1013)

After the frenzy of activity at the turn of the millennium, Æthelred appears to have left military affairs to his ealdormen and local officials from 1003-05. It is unclear if this was an intentional policy or if local leaders were forced to respond by necessity. As mentioned earlier, pirate fleets could appear and disappear long before a national army could assemble — or even before word could reach the king, should he be stationed at the opposite end of the country. The kingdom Æthelred had to defend was far larger than that ruled by Alfred the Great a century earlier. And beyond that, it is worth noting that Anglo-Saxon kings did not maintain standing armies on a permanent basis, so keeping national levies raised "just in case" would have been both expensive and extremely unpopular. While the nucleus of late Saxon armies could include sworn, professional soldiers (like the famed "housecarls" of Harold II), the vast majority of forces were made up of regular Anglo-Saxons who had to leave their farms and livelihoods to march. With this in mind, it is easy to see why Æthelred relied so heavily on mercenaries throughout his reign.

That said, from the mid-1000s on, Viking raids continued and Æthelred's nobles failed to effectively oppose them. Despite recording some isolated victories, the annalist also writes of treachery, assassinations, and chaos among the English during these years. An even greater foe threatened from outside the realm: Sweyn Forkbeard, the king of Denmark, who first becomes prominent in the *Chronicle* during these years. He would dominate the military landscape for a decade to come.

King Sweyn Arrives (1003-04)

Despite the tribute paid in 1002, the *Chronicle* records more Viking attacks throughout 1003, led by Sweyn Forkbeard. He had ruled Denmark since 986, when he overthrew his father, Harald Bluetooth. Sweyn had also been King of Norway since the same year, except for a period from 995-1000 when Olaf Tryggvason usurped the throne during his bloody wars of conversion. Sweyn's motivation for invading England in 1003 may simply have been glory and riches, but other suggestions have been put forward. A common interpretation is that Sweyn's invasion was revenge for St. Brice's Day. It is also possible that Sweyn resented Æthelred after the English king had confirmed Olaf as a Christian; the confirmation had sparked Olaf's crusading frenzy throughout Sweyn's territory, which only ended with Olaf's death in battle in 1000. Either way, for several years Æthelred's divide and conquer plan had worked, but with Sweyn back in control of Norway, the Scandinavian overlord was free to visit England's shores.

Sweyn's men sacked the city of Exeter in 1003. Rather than attribute the city's fall to Sweyn's might, the chronicler blames Exeter on a Frenchman named Hugh. Queen Emma, Æthelred's new wife, had placed Hugh in the city as a reeve, but the *Chronicle* does not say how Hugh caused or allowed the sacking of Exeter. We only know that after the city was looted and destroyed, a regional army gathered to stop Sweyn's destruction. It was led by Ealdorman Ælfric of Hampshire, who seems to have been restored to power since betraying Æthelred in 992. The chronicler describes Ælfric back in 992 as someone in whom "the king had most trust." In 1003, though, he is "up to his old tricks," confirming that this is indeed the same Ælfric from a decade earlier. In 1003, when he should have given his men an example of bravery and leadership, Ælfric instead "pretended to vomit, saying he was ill" when faced with Sweyn's army. It is, of course, possible that Ælfric's illness was real, brought on by pre-battle apprehension and terror. But given Ælfric's prior treachery, the annalist gives him no breaks. When Sweyn saw the low morale of the English army, surely weakened by the ealdorman's real or feigned illness, he burned down the village of Wilton. The *Chronicle* does not record any battle between Sweyn and Ælfric; it seems that given the sorry state of Ælfric's army, Sweyn was content to simply ignore the English forces, pillaging towns instead of risking his men's lives in pitched battle. From 1003 on, this policy of avoidance on both sides would become more and more common.

In 1004, Sweyn sacked Norwich, prompting a regional leader named Ulfcytel the Bold to confront him shortly after. Ulfcytel's men first attempted to destroy the Vikings' ships. After this failed, Ulfcytel's East Anglian army blocked Sweyn's men from returning to the shore. They collided in a fierce battle that seems to have been a success for the English. Despite the deaths of many East Anglian nobles, no more raiding or pillaging is recorded for 1004, and by 1005, Sweyn was gone. The *Chronicle*, ever eager to portray the English leadership in a negative light, laments that the Vikings would have been completely destroyed if the army had been "at their full strength." The heavy losses at the hands of Ulfcytel, along with a severe famine, prompted a break in the fighting when Sweyn left for Denmark in 1005.

Routing the Scots and Killing Ælfhelm (1006)

In 1006, England was weakened by years of war and the recent famine. But even with the Vikings gone, there would be no rest for the English. The Scots began raiding in Northumbria, perhaps aware that with the Vikings gone it was their turn to exploit the weakened Anglo-Saxons. When this army, sent by Malcolm II of Scotland, marched south, it was met with indifference by local Saxon leaders. Men like Ælfhelm, the Ealdorman of York, would have been expected to confront the Scots. However, it seems that no defense was forthcoming, so another local man took action: Uhtred, the son of a local lord. Uhtred's father, according to a text called *De obsessione Dunelmi*,[62] was too old to fight, so Uhtred stepped in and boldly confronted the intruding Scottish forces. His men routed the Scots, with local women paid to wash the heads of the Scots and put them on poles. As a reward for putting a swift end to the raiding, King Æthelred granted Uhtred governorship of all Northumbria, despite the fact that Uhtred's father still lived and that men like Ælfhelm held power there.

These details all come from *De obsessione*, but the *Chronicle* does record the murder of Ælfhelm in 1006 (along with the blinding of his sons), perhaps paving the way for Uhtred to succeed to the whole territory. *De obsessione* is an extremely valuable source, but it is problematic in one regard: it places these events in the year 968. Æthelred, Uhtred, and Malcolm would have been far too young to participate, if Uhtred had even been born yet. However, historians have managed to correct this error thanks to the details of another source, the *Annals of Ulster*, which records a Scottish raid into Northumbria in 1006. If the details of *De obsessione* are moved to 1006, its main players are all in power. Then, when combined with the *Chronicle*'s entry for 1006, it appears that Uhtred would indeed have been able to succeed to all Northumbria with Ælfhelm dead. This hodgepodge of sources actually manages to create a relatively straightforward account of English military politics in 1006: Ælfhelm fails to oppose raiders and suddenly meets a grisly end. Uhtred is willing to fight, so he is awarded all of Northumbria.[63]

There may, of course, have been other motives for killing Ælfhelm, such as suspected disloyalty. The king had already proven himself willing to attack those whose allegiance was suspect, such as his raids on Rochester in

986 or the wholesale killing of Danes in 1002. A later version of the *Chronicle* gives more detail regarding the murder of Ælfhelm. Known as the *Worcester Chronicle*, this version accuses a new leader named Eadric Streona ("the Grasper") for Ælfhelm's demise. Eadric and his family would experience a meteoric rise to power in the following years, so the implication here is that Eadric was doing King Æthelred's dirty work in exchange for titles and wealth.[64] This same account directly accuses Æthelred of blinding Ælfhelm's two sons shortly afterwards.

If we are willing to believe that Eadric was indeed the one behind the assassination, and that Æthelred ordered the blinding, then again we have a very clear picture of a king who would stop at nothing to enforce his military standards. Even if the later addition is ignored, suspicion should still fall directly on Æthelred; he had mutilated the offspring of military traitors before, and we have no indication that anyone was ever punished for the killing. In all likelihood, Æthelred made an example of Ælfhelm and left his sons maimed as a warning. In fact, this view has become the status quo position among historians of Æthelred's reign. Keynes and Lavelle, for example, have little trouble believing that events unfolded this way.[65] If this is the case, then as in 993, Æthelred made his point in the most ruthless way possible. Showing disloyalty or cowardice in the face of an enemy could be punished by death — and by the mutilation of kin. Clearly this was not the Æthelred of Ribman's play, holed up in a monastery, waiting for the end. This was a king willing to depose and kill his regional leaders in order to find someone willing to lead an army.

The Autumn Campaigns (1006)

Despite the relative success of Uhtred in the north, the *Chronicle* reports that the Vikings had returned by midsummer. Æthelred promptly ordered out "all the levies from Wessex and Mercia" and the English armies pursued the Vikings all autumn, but failed to meet them in battle. The presence of both foreign and native armies caused hardship for the English, with the *Chronicle* noting that "neither the home levies nor the invading host did them any good!" [66]

While unsuccessful in opposing the invaders, the autumn campaigns of 1006 still show a burst of decisiveness that the king had lacked in the previous few years. The campaigns also suggest that Æthelred viewed the efforts of his local magnates as insufficient, finally intervening. Although the *Chronicle* does not specify if Æthelred was with the army this time, its organization and deployment trace back to him.

Although Æthelred may well have led this force — we simply aren't told — a prominent writer of the period still defended Æthelred's decision to delegate generalship when necessary. Noting that the king had good precedent for not personally accompanying every army, Abbot Ælfric the Homilist concluded that this practice was acceptable so long as the men leading the army were worthy.[67] The implication here is obviously that many times, as this chapter will bear out, the king did not select worthy men; however, in advocating for war and selecting which armies to accompany, Æthelred was doing nothing inherently wrong or "un-kingly."

After an entire season where the two armies managed to avoid each other, the English levies were finally dismissed. The Vikings made their winter camp on the Isle of Wight, but soon ventured "more than fifty miles inland," destroying Wallingford. The *Chronicle* then records a battle between the Vikings and a local force from East Kennet, but the English are defeated; we are not told who led this local resistance. Then the king made peace with the invaders, sending them tribute and provisions — as before, not as a solution, but only after military force had failed numerous times.

King Æthelred's Great Fleet (1008-09)

In 1007 and 1008, England was free from attack. The tribute payment, "distasteful as it [was]," had done its job.[68] Æthelred was not idle during this time, though, and seems to have recognized the growing crisis that faced his nation. He tried a tactic he had used a decade and a half earlier by constructing a new navy. Now in his early 40s, the king again ordered the construction of a fleet with help from the entire nation. By 1009, the fleet was ready and the *Chronicle* marvels that it was more massive than any fleet "in the reign of any king," with Æthelred himself present to see it off. However, when the ships assembled at Sandwich that year, fickle nobles again ruined the king's plans. A minor lord named Wulfnoth Cild ("Child") was accused of treason and immediately fled with 20 of the king's ships.[69] In response, 80 ships were sent after him, but a storm destroyed these vessels. With 100 ships now gone, "the effort of the whole nation" had been wasted. The *Chronicle* then grows dismissive, stating that the king and his leading men "went home" after the catastrophic turn of events.

Although the fleet is sometimes misinterpreted as having been completely destroyed in the chaos, this was not the case. Despite the stunning loss of 100 vessels to infighting, the *Chronicle* notes that the remaining ships returned to London. In commanding 80 ships to chase the treacherous Wulfnoth, Æthelred was again doing what any active king would — attempting to punish those who had betrayed him. The storm that fell upon the pursuers can only be described as bad luck, but Æthelred may have perceived it as something far more alarming. If he had ever wondered if he and his kingdom were cursed, those thoughts may have been most prominent from 1009 onward. As Abels writes, "Æthelred had been taught by his ecclesiastical tutors that the physical conditions of his kingdom and its people reflected God's favour or wrath... a king and his people who failed to act justly and show due reverence to the Church could expect divine punishment."[70] The theme of faith, penance, and divine wrath is also one of the primary focuses of Roach's book.

The king now had to turn his attention back to worldly matters and make do with what was left, and he seems to have made an effective job of it: stationing the remaining ships in London was a strategic move, not a despondent show of defeat. London was the key to England, and notably was the assembly point for the previous fleet in 992. The city had been repeatedly attacked or re-conquered over the previous centuries: the *Chronicle* alone records attacks in 839, 851, 886, and 994 and would record them again later in 1009, as well as in 1013 and 1016.[71] A Norse saga, which will be discussed in depth later, also records an attack on London in 1014.[72] Guarding the Thames may actually have been the best way to utilize the fleet, especially if it was a mere remnant of what it had been. Obviously, Æthelred's plans had gone awry, but he was not too immobilized to salvage some use out of his fleet.

Thorkell's Host vs Æthelred's National Army (1009)

Another Viking fleet arrived in England in 1009, this one led by Thorkell the Tall. Thanks to later sagas and traditions, Thorkell is now as much myth as man, so little is known about his exact historical background. However, he seems to have been the leader of a fierce and semi-legendary order of fighters called the *Jomsvikings*; these professional soldiers supposedly lived by a strict code that forbade them from showing fear or fleeing from battle. Thorkell's men would torment the English for the next few years, kicking off their campaign by quickly subduing the English in Kent. The *Chronicle* reports that local leaders "made peace" with the raiders before too much damage could be done, paying them a tribute of 3,000 pounds. The actions of the Kentish leaders also reveal that Æthelred was not the only Englishman paying for peace during this era.

Immediately following the fall of Kent, Thorkell's men occupied the Isle of Wight. Then King Æthelred "order[ed] out levies from the entire nation," showing that even if the fleet had met with disaster and more Vikings had arrived, he had not given up.[73] The king seemed determined to confront the Vikings in 1009, whether by land or sea, and personally led this national force. If the army from 1006 had failed to find the Vikings, this one would be different. The *Chronicle* says that "the king surrounded them with all the levies when they were making for their ships." The *Chronicle*'s wording here is interesting because the Vikings are already retreating to the shore when Æthelred finds them. Perhaps they were simply loading their boats with treasure, but other possibilities are at least worth a mention: the raiders may have been reeling from an earlier, unrecorded defeat in this episode, but a more likely possibility is that they were pursuing a policy of avoidance once again. It was probably well-advised to avoid the king's national army at all costs, instead plundering easier targets.

Then Eadric Streona, who was by this time Ealdorman of Mercia, "prevented" the king from attacking. Again, note that the *Chronicle* does not blame the king — it actually gives him credit for trapping the Vikings — but a regional leader instead. However, even if the *Chronicle* rushes to judge Eadric, there may have been very rational reasons for persuading the king not to attack. The most obvious is that the English may have been in a poor strategic position against a more skilled opponent.

The annalist is quick to make Eadric Streona the scapegoat for nearly everything that goes wrong for the English from this point on — it almost seems like the chronicler paints Eadric as a double-agent, working craftily behind the scenes to undermine his own nation. This is where it is important to remember that the chronicler's opinion was formed with the benefit of hindsight. In 1009, Æthelred had no reason to believe Eadric sought to undermine him, and in fact, may have had positive evidence to the contrary. Remember that the writer of the *Worcester Chronicle* (although also writing with hindsight) paints Eadric as loyal to the point of murdering Ælfhelm for the benefit of the king. Eadric's willingness to act as enforcer — as well as his low birth — made him, in reality, the king's greatest ally. Eadric, despite holding all of Mercia under his sway by 1009, did not come from a notable family. He had been "made" by Æthelred. Any thoughts that Eadric was actively trying to harm his king at this point are not just hasty, but completely implausible; with no family birthright to speak of, Eadric's very position and power depended on the continuing favor of the king. That said, at Eadric's advice, the king did not engage the raiding army — but the *Chronicle* again has only given us a one-sided view of the event. As with earlier military campaigns, failure is ascribed to misfortune or foolishness on the English side. The Vikings are virtually never given credit for their successes, making it sound like their victories are caused solely by English mistakes. Thorkell's Vikings, fierce as they were, likewise declined to fight Æthelred's national army — the policy of avoidance ran strong on both sides.

That winter, the king's earlier foresight to send the fleet to London paid off. Thorkell's forces made frequent attacks on London at this time, but "always suffered heavy losses there."[74] Soon they left, attacking another *burh* and succeeding, burning Oxford. However, the *Chronicle* says that from that point on, the invaders specifically avoided London because "the levies" would oppose them there — presumably the king's same national army from earlier, as well as the ships. Although Oxford and the Isle of

Wight fell prey to the Vikings, Æthelred had succeeded in protecting England's most valuable city, if nothing else.

Thorkell's Trail of Fire (1010-11)

If 1009 had seen some mixed success on the part of the English, the events of 1010 and 1011 would be different. The *Chronicle* records a dire situation throughout the country during these years. At this point, the more traditional view of a country on the verge of collapse finally begins to hold weight. Before 1010, there had always been some form of effective resistance and retaliation — raids into the northwest, attacks on Normandy, strong stands by local leaders — but by 1010 Thorkell's host seems to have finally worn down the English. In addition, while many of the previous Viking raids were small scale (like those in the early 980s) or only affected certain areas (like the bands from the late 990s), Thorkell would soon occupy huge swaths of England.

In early 1010, after recuperating and making repairs on their ships, Thorkell's host sprung back into action. According to the *Chronicle*, they heard that Ulfcytel — the same leader who had valiantly resisted Sweyn Forkbeard in 1004 — had raised an army. Thorkell rushed to confront him, no longer wishing to avoid the English forces. The two sides met in battle, but "the East Anglians soon took to flight," and many nobles fell during the fighting. Now in control of East Anglia, Thorkell spent the spring and summer burning and terrorizing the countryside, "slaying men and cattle, and burning through the fens." Countless settlements were burned down at this time and the English armies failed to confront them. The *Chronicle* notes, with obvious hyperbole, that "when the enemy was in the east, then our levies were mustered in the west; and when they were in the south, then our levies were in the north." Although Æthelred's advisors and generals had been repeatedly blamed over the preceding entries, in 1010 we get some of our first direct criticism of the king: "Then all the councillors were summoned to the king, for a plan for the defence of the realm had to be devised then and there, but whatever course of action was decided upon... was not followed for even a single month." Then resistance finally seems to have collapsed. Earlier in 1010, men like Ulfcytel had raised levies and the *Chronicle* likewise implies that armies had been mustered throughout the summer and fall. By the end of 1010, though, the annalist comments that "no leader... was willing to raise levies, but each fled as quickly as he could." The wave of violence continued on through the winter, with Thorkell destroying the land by fire.

By 1011, Thorkell controlled virtually all of southern and eastern England ("East Anglia, Essex, Oxfordshire, Cambridgeshire, Hertfordshire, Buckinghamshire, Bedfordshire, half of Huntingdonshire... all of Kent, and Sussex... the district around Hastings, and Surrey, and Berkshire, and Hampshire, and a great part of Wiltshire").[75]

Æthelred had remained firmly in control of his kingdom for nearly 35 years, but his power and influence must have experienced a rapid decline during Thorkell's occupation. Æthelred was king in name, but much of his country now fell under the rule of the Vikings. Then the king and his advisors "craved peace," offering Thorkell a tribute. The *Chronicle* goes on to criticize not the payment itself, but its timing, noting that "tribute was not offered them in time, but when they had done their worst." Thorkell's men spent the rest of 1011 harassing and killing the English inhabitants, "notwithstanding all this truce and peace and tribute." The Vikings also took several nobles and clergymen captive at this time, probably hoping to ransom them off and further enrich themselves. One of these prisoners, Archbishop Ælfheah of Canterbury, would be involved in one of the war's great turning points the next year.

Thorkell Joins Æthelred (1012)

In 1012, when Archbishop Ælfheah would not let himself be ransomed, the Vikings drunkenly murdered him by "pelting him to death with bones and the heads of cattle."[76] Shortly after this, with the tribute fully paid, the Vikings dispersed. Æthelred's next action, though, was to turn Thorkell from foe to friend, employing him to defend England against rival Vikings. Thorkell's motivation for defecting to Æthelred has piqued the curiosity of historians for centuries, with several possibilities typically put forth. A common interpretation is that Thorkell felt remorseful for the savage way the archbishop had been killed, which had not been his intention. Another frequent interpretation is that Thorkell sensed he was losing control over his drunken soldiers; thus, he defected to the English with the core of his forces. That said, it is also possible that the king simply made a good offer. With the tribute paid and most of the raiders on their way home, Thorkell would have had nothing substantial left to do. Fighting for the English would be a way to secure further payment and stay busy.

Either way, the *Chronicle* reports that 45 of Thorkell's ships defected to Æthelred, "on the condition he clothe and feed them."[77] If Englishmen would not fight effectively or remain loyal to Æthelred, he would employ professionals who would. Æthelred's use of Thorkell may appear desperate, but the king had already seen his military plans thwarted several times by his own nobles. Thorkell was also the perfect man for the job — no Viking had conquered more of England to that point, and now he had not only been neutralized, but would be the king's own defender. The hiring of Thorkell shows that Æthelred was willing to defend his country by any means necessary, using his vast wealth to hire some of the fiercest warriors available.

Defending London (1013)

After a year of peace, Thorkell's services were needed in August 1013, when Sweyn returned. However, unlike many of the previous invasions, Sweyn started his campaign in the north, perhaps because Thorkell was with Æthelred in the south. The northern English offered up no resistance. Uhtred and the Northumbrians quickly made peace with Sweyn, submitting to him, as did the people of Lindsey (Lincolnshire). This ripple effect carried through the rest of the kingdom, with Oxfordshire, the Five Boroughs, and even Winchester — the traditional heartland of the House of Wessex — submitting to Sweyn without a fight.[78] Æthelred's kingdom had contracted to a small core around London by the end of 1013. With little remaining support after Sweyn's whirlwind campaign, Æthelred was now in imminent danger. Even with the rest of the kingdom defeated, Æthelred remained in London, apparently willing to fight with his last loyal citizens until the end. Clearly he was not foolish or cowardly, as William of Malmesbury would concede years later.[79]

Soon Sweyn closed in. He tried to take London, but the *Chronicle* says the city refused to submit because of Æthelred and Thorkell's presence. Æthelred and his defender fought on, rallying the Londoners until Sweyn was repelled. If Æthelred could be accused of avoiding direct military conflict in the preceding few years, his defense of London in 1013 was a prominent exception. Fleeing was an option, especially with Thorkell's ships at his disposal. Æthelred chose to stay and fight, and he succeeded — at least for the time being.

With his efforts thwarted, Sweyn left. He headed west and received formal submission from many English lords. With nearly the entire nation under Sweyn's control, the *Chronicle* says that he was now the "undisputed" (sometimes translated "full") king of England, despite Æthelred's inconvenient presence in London.

The Fall of London and Exile (1013)

When Sweyn returned to London a second time, the morale of Æthelred's men plummeted. The Londoners finally gave in to Sweyn's persistence, submitting out of sheer fear, according to the *Chronicle*. Only then did Æthelred escape, perhaps utilizing Thorkell's ships. Then Æthelred sent his wife Emma, and their sons Alfred and Edward, away to Normandy. Æthelred himself seems to have stayed behind for a time, tarrying in the Thames with the ships despite London's fall. Perhaps he spent these dangerous days in negotiation, as the *Chronicle* claims that both Sweyn and Thorkell demanded payment from him. He was not captured or harmed, however, so it seems likely that he secured some kind of agreement with Thorkell.

Then Æthelred sailed to the Isle of Wight, alarmingly close to the mainland, celebrating Christmas there. While the Isle of Wight was the final place to show Æthelred hospitality, they must have been eager to get him off the island; surely they did not want to incur Sweyn's wrath. With the loss of his crown and the passing of the winter solstice, these must have been some of Æthelred's darkest hours, literally and figuratively. While his hesitant departure from England may have had practical motives (such as seeing how much support he had on the Isle of Wight, or recovering treasure), Æthelred may also have lingered simply because there was no guarantee he would ever set foot in England again. Perhaps this is reading too much into our scant sources, but sometimes historians tend to forget that the names they study belonged to real, living people who had emotions as vivid and deep as ours. While distant rulers often acted with political motivations, there is no reason to assume they did not also act out of emotion or sentimentality. Æthelred's slow withdrawal from England stands in sharp contrast to the hurried exiles of his wife and sons. Given the total collapse of his support, Æthelred now faced the very real possibility of living out his days in France and being buried on foreign soil. He seems to have spent as long as possible in or near his former nation, whether it was borne from an empty sadness or one last, bitter show of defiance.

Finally, after Christmas, Æthelred left for Normandy after a reign of 35 years. It had been the longest tenure of any Saxon king of England. He took shelter at Richard II's court, joining Emma and his younger sons. Even if Æthelred's marriage to Emma of Normandy had not been especially helpful against the Vikings, at this moment it was fortunate that her brother Richard was just across the channel. Although Æthelred seems to have finally acknowledged that he was not safe in England by the end of 1013, he had not gone down easily. He had held his kingdom through three decades of Viking attack — and soon he would get a chance to redeem himself.

CHAPTER FIVE

TRIUMPHANT RETURN AND ILLNESS (1014-16)

The deposed Æthelred spent the winter of 1013-14 in Normandy with his family, with Sweyn still recognized as "full king" in England. In February 1014, though, luck was finally on Æthelred's side: Sweyn died.[80] Despite being the first foreigner to ever usurp the English crown, Sweyn is practically unknown outside of Scandinavia today. His five-week reign is the shortest of any English monarch, allowing for the possible exception of Lady Jane Grey.[81] So while Sweyn Forkbeard is widely renowned as a legendary Viking commander and a long-reigning king of Denmark, virtually nothing survives from his brief time as ruler of England. He is the English equivalent of William Henry Harrison, the American whose 31-day term as president has become a source of amusement, overshadowing a long and storied life. Sweyn's young son Canute, probably no more than 20 years old, was then proclaimed king by the

Viking fleet. He had been present with his father during the conquest, gaining valuable experience, and surely he assumed the kingdom was naturally his.

In Wessex, however, the English *witan* — the councilors — decided to do something completely different. They chose to recall Æthelred and negotiate his restoration to the throne, "if only he would govern more justly" because "no lord was dearer to them than their rightful lord."[82] The councilors who recalled Æthelred understood that they had the upper hand — if they ever wanted to change the way a ruler behaved and governed, now was the time. The *Chronicle*'s wording is noteworthy, though, because Æthelred's military and defensive abilities are not criticized — his sense of justice is. Yet again, this flies in the face of the traditional narrative; Æthelred was not a poor ruler because he had lost the fight against the Vikings, but because he was perceived as personally unjust. Perhaps the *witan* had men like Eadric Streona in mind, the king's close ally who had orchestrated purges on his behalf.

Either way, Æthelred was the man they wanted in power, not Canute. The councilors would have also considered Æthelred's eldest sons, Æthelstan and Edmund, who had seemingly remained in England.[83] By 1014, they would have been well into adulthood, probably eager to assume leadership responsibilities. As discussed in the first chapter, the *witan* could technically elect a less-legitimate or less-obvious candidate; it had happened to Æthelred in 975 when his less-legitimate older brother, Edward, was elected instead of him. In more extreme cases, sons could leapfrog their already-crowned fathers or the kingdom could be formally divided among family members, with two legitimate kings.[84] To say that the Anglo-Saxons created written, formal laws of succession like those of the Tudors would be anachronistic. The main point to understand for Æthelred is this: his invitation to return on Sweyn's death was not the least bit guaranteed, especially with his eldest sons still in the country — yet he was the one offered the crown.

As with his departure from England, Æthelred's return — at least at first — was calculated and methodical. Upon receiving word that the *witan* wanted him back, Æthelred sent his son Edward (who was probably about 12) to England with a favorable response. Æthelred agreed that he would "remedy each of the things that they all abhorred" and would forgive those who had turned against him.[85] This is the first agreement between an English king and his people recorded in writing, making it something of an "Anglo-Saxon Magna Carta."[86] Æthelred could not have known his constitutional legacy, though. For him, it meant a chance to retake his kingdom, and for his nobles, it meant that they would be safe from retribution. The *Chronicle* goes out of its way to record Æthelred's "forgiveness," suggesting the English were worried about the destruction a vindictive Æthelred could bring if let back in. They were right: Æthelred would return with a vengeance and retake the rest of his kingdom by force.

Attack on London Bridge (1014)

That spring, Æthelred was reinstated as king, coming "home to his own people." His return was apparently a happy event for those who had deserted him just a few months prior: he was "received with joy by them all."[87] Much of the country still belonged to the Vikings, however, now under the command of Canute.

According to the *Saga of Olaf Haraldsson*, Æthelred's first decision upon returning was to recapture London. Now back in charge, he immediately "sent an invitation to all the men who would enter into his pay, to join him in recovering the country."[88] Among the many soldiers Æthelred recruited was the Viking mercenary Olaf Haraldsson, who commanded a force of his own. The *Saga* reports that Æthelred "ordered a great assault" on London but that Canute's men bravely held out.[89] Æthelred then held council with his men to decide his next plan of action, where Olaf devised a plan to pull down London Bridge, which was lined with Danish warriors. By tying ropes around the bridge's supports and rowing backwards, with thatched roofs shielding the boats, the bridge toppled down. Like with Thorkell before, Æthelred had hired a professional to help him militarily, and if the account is genuine, the tactic worked. Following the bridge's collapse, Canute's men "became afraid," and submitted to Æthelred.

While this episode is not mentioned in the *Chronicle*, some scholars have advocated for its veracity. Jan Ragnar Hagland and Bruce Watson argue that "there is no reason to disbelieve [the] account of the attack on London Bridge. It has a very plausible context within the turbulent history of this period."[90] However, the *Saga* is a much later source that probably was not written down until the 12th or 13th centuries, with numerous later versions soon following. The *Saga* also includes several other details about England and Æthelred not found in the *Chronicle*. It says that Olaf was charged with defending the country from attack, staying with Æthelred for three years. Olaf was also responsible for reconquering remaining territories still held by Canute, apparently fighting against Ulfcytel the Bold and extracting tribute from other regions of the kingdom. It also implies that Sweyn died during autumn, not winter, and as the result of a ghostly scare — St. Edmund of East Anglia apparently frightened Sweyn to death.[91]

Although it might sound like this dramatic saga has little in common with the *Chronicle*'s account of 1014, that is not the case. The *Saga* and the *Chronicle* agree on numerous fundamental details. The *Saga* correctly notes that Sweyn had conquered England, but died soon after, passing leadership onto his son, Canute. They agree on Æthelred's place of exile ("Valland," which Snorri uses to refer to Normandy), the names of his sons, and even which regional rulers were present during the era (like Ulfcytel the Bold). The *Saga* also lines up with what we know about Æthelred's behavior from the *Chronicle*: he favored the use of Viking mercenaries, had ships at his disposal (from Thorkell and his own fleets), held council before making important decisions, and placed special emphasis on London throughout his reign. It is important to remember that medieval sources often contradict themselves on even the smallest details and are prone to placing historical figures in the wrong places at the wrong times or giving entirely different accounts of the same event. *De obsessione*, discussed in the last chapter, is a good example of this, and yet historians have still managed to salvage something out of it. Not all details from the *Saga* concerning England are corroborated by the *Chronicle*, of course, and it was composed later; we can never be sure of its complete reliability.

That said, if Æthelred and Olaf's attack on London is a later fabrication, then it is an extremely convincing one. It gets numerous details right about the state of England, Æthelred, and Æthelred's known behavior. In all likelihood, even if Olaf did not really stay with Æthelred for three years or battle Ulfcytel, a confrontation at London probably did take place. The *Chronicle* even notes that Æthelred controlled London again by 1016 (and probably before that), even though it was occupied by Sweyn the last time it was referenced. Æthelred somehow regained control of London between 1014 and 1016, and since London was in such a defensible position, he would have used military force to reclaim it. It is virtually impossible that Canute would have left such an important city undefended. Again, a daring attack by Æthelred in 1014 fits snugly within this framework.

More importantly for Æthelred's military reputation, the *Saga* shows the king independently of the English tradition, which was already well on its way to molding him into a caricature by the 12th and 13th centuries. Instead, Æthelred is active and present in the *Saga*, commanding "great assaults" and recruiting seasoned warriors to fight with him. The *Saga* acknowledges that the king had been kicked out of his own country, but still has no qualms about showing him using force and taking swift military action.

Whether the *Saga* is to be fully believed or not, Æthelred did return and his momentum only grew from there.

Attacking Canute and
Destroying Lindsey (1014)

Æthelred's next action is recorded in the *Chronicle*, though, and shows him using similar vigor. Despite being the oldest English king in nearly a century, Æthelred did not rest after his voyage back to England and probable battle at London.[92] He decided to face the upstart Canute head on. Wood even remarks that Æthelred seemed bolstered by "a new enthusiasm for military affairs."[93] Æthelred quickly marched his army north to Lindsey, Canute's de facto headquarters.[94] The *Chronicle* says that Canute had reached an agreement with the men of Lindsey and that they all planned to "set out together and harry" the land. This setup is important because it provides the rationale for Æthelred's impending attack. The citizens of Lindsey were the ones to blame, not the king. The chronicler thus avoids a contradiction between the king's restoration agreement and his plan to attack fellow Englishmen. In the chronicler's view, due to Lindsey's disloyalty, Æthelred was entirely justified in leading an army north into Viking-held territory. The *Chronicle* says that Æthelred attacked Canute with his army at "full strength," and that "they made raids and burned and slew every human being they could find." His attack forced Canute out to sea. Canute fled back to Denmark after dropping off English hostages at Sandwich. Despite the later reputations of Æthelred and Canute, their roles seem reversed here; Canute was the unready one, caught off guard by Æthelred's decisive action. In just a few weeks, Æthelred had reconquered his kingdom. His restoration agreement had opened the door for his return, but he had done the rest of the work.

He was not a Henry VI, bewildered and helpless, placed back on the throne by forces outside his control. Æthelred directly involved himself, leading massive armies against his enemies and succeeding (probably more than once, thanks to details from the *Saga*). He had made a powerful statement: the kingdom was his again, and those who did not recognize it would suffer.

Following Æthelred's triumphant return in 1014, peace and stability were brief. His heir, Æthelstan, died in 1014, perhaps wounded in the earlier battles. Then political infighting began again when Eadric Streona, still doing the king's dirty work, had two northern nobles murdered in 1015.[95] Æthelred's failure to punish the crimes implies that the assassinations were carried out on his orders, or at least that he was happy to turn a blind eye. His subjects may have seen this as a clear violation of Æthelred's restoration agreement, where the king had promised to put old grudges aside. Æthelred's new heir presumptive, Edmund, seized on the outrage his father had caused by setting himself up as an independent ruler farther north,[96] even marrying the widow of Sigeferth, one of the assassinated nobles. After the brief period of unity following Æthelred's victories in 1014, by 1015 that unity had fractured again. Edmund had essentially seceded and Æthelred was acting in ways his subjects must have seen as erratic or tyrannical.

Sadly, Æthelred's reign had achieved a kind of symmetry by 1015: it had started with a wave of explosive factions and now it was ending the same way (it is important to remember that this observation is only possible with hindsight — Æthelred may not have known he was near the end of his life). While tumultuous factions had been present throughout the entire reign, they now ruptured the bonds between king and people at the least convenient time — Canute was back with a fresh army.

Illness, Delegation of the Army, and Betrayal (1015)

Canute's army landed on the southern coast and quickly overran parts of Dorset, Wiltshire, and Somerset. Æthelred was nearby at this time, at a royal manor in Cosham, but could not respond to Canute's new invasion: midway through 1015, the *Chronicle* records that "the king was laying sick at Cosham." This is significant, because the *Chronicle* is almost always silent about illnesses. Even the serious stomach ailments of Alfred and Eadred are only found in other sources. More often, the *Chronicle* simply reports that kings died, offering no explanation. So for Æthelred's illness to be mentioned, it was probably both well-known and incapacitating. To make matters worse, Æthelred was already old by Anglo-Saxon standards. Novelist Patricia Bracewell, who features Æthelred in her historical fiction, puts it best: "That the *Chronicle* actually notes that he was sick that autumn of 1015 is an indication of how grave his condition must have been... at 47-ish, Æthelred was well past his 'sell-by' date in comparison to his forebears, and any illness would have been worrisome."[97] With Æthelred ill, leadership of the army had to be delegated to someone else. The king was too sick to move to a defensible city, much less command an army.

It seems that Eadric was the man Æthelred trusted as his general, because later that year, Eadric raised levies and met with Edmund's forces from "the north."[98] It is tempting to interpret this as one, unified English army with troops from all over the country, but the kingdom was still divided at this time. Edmund even began issuing charters in his own name as "King-Prince Edmund" around this time. Although the exact context is unclear, this careful phrasing could be indicative of Edmund's rebellion and the fragile state of English unity during 1015 and 1016.[99] The king's faction, led by Eadric, met with Edmund's rebel faction not as part of any national, united army, but as two rival cliques combining to fight a common foe. This uneasy alliance quickly disintegrated, apparently because Eadric sought to betray Edmund. Whether it was really Eadric's fault or not, the separation of the two armies is hardly surprising; Edmund and Eadric were unlikely allies and each had reason to hate and fear the other. Edmund was married to the widow of a man Eadric had killed, after all.

After this failed meeting with Prince Edmund, Eadric defected to the Vikings. The *Chronicle* says that he "won over forty ships from their allegiance to the king" and submitted to Canute. The loss of 40 more ships must have been devastating news for the king, especially since they had been stolen by the man he trusted most. Æthelred had raised Eadric up from obscurity just a decade earlier, but from a self-preservation standpoint, Eadric's betrayal made sense. Eadric's lone protector was Æthelred, who was old and sick. For Eadric, maybe it seemed better to throw his lot in with Canute while he still could, rather than risk the vengeance of Edmund, who would likely take the king's place soon.

The Final Campaign of King Æthelred (1016)

Eadric and Canute ravaged the land all winter. By early 1016, with Æthelred sick and Eadric playing for the other team, resistance against the Vikings fell to Edmund. He tried to rally the loyalists in early 1016, but the soldiers refused to campaign unless Æthelred — now in London — was with them. Perhaps they wanted to be sure Æthelred approved of Edmund's actions in light of the prince's recent rebellion. Maybe they wanted the morale boost of being led by their anointed king, or maybe they still had the triumphs of 1014 in mind. Either way, Æthelred was obviously still important to his citizens. Edmund asked his father to join him with the Londoners and Æthelred agreed, leading an army out. However, the *Chronicle* then says that Æthelred was warned of treachery and returned to London, where he died a few weeks later.

The accusation that Æthelred fled solely due to treachery has been scrutinized in recent years. Traitors may have been in his midst, but Lavelle suggests that the king's retreat probably had more to do with illness, wondering if it wasn't "the action of an exhausted man."[100] Circumstantial evidence also points in this direction.[101] Leading the army was the king's only recorded action between his illness and his death. Most likely, Æthelred was physically unable to handle the rigors of campaigning any longer and withdrew to London, where he died.

This final act can tell us one last point about Æthelred, and one that parallels his reign as a whole: the king was willing to try even if he did not find success. Leading an army out while dying shows considerable resolve, and suggests that he still understood the significance of leading his men in person. Edmund needed Æthelred to personally "hand the baton" to him and Æthelred obliged, even while sick.

Intentionally or not, our most famous image of King Æthelred mirrors this image of a worn-out, but battle-tested defender. A portrait of Æthelred from the Abingdon version of the *Chronicle* shows him on his throne, a magnificent sword in hand and a crown resting on his head. His hair is splotched with streaks of gray and his face is worried and wrinkled. The painting comes from a later copy, probably from the 1200s, so it is not an eye-witness drawing of Æthelred's actual likeness. That said, perhaps there is some truth to that image, at least symbolically — the actions of Æthelred from 1014-16 very much mirror this depiction of an aging, concerned monarch who nonetheless fought on with considerable energy, especially considering his deteriorating condition. The *Chronicle* likewise recognizes Æthelred's many efforts over the years when it marks his passing: "He ended his days on St. George's Day, after a life of much hardship and many difficulties." England in 1016 was in crisis again, but Æthelred had held on until the end.

CONCLUSION

Æthelred's kingdom would not survive him long. Edmund, like his father, found initial success against Canute and his allies. He quickly assumed leadership of the remaining loyalists in the wake of his father's death, raising levies to oppose Canute. King Edmund seemed to have had much less difficulty recruiting men than when he had been acting on his father's behalf. In a sweeping campaign, Edmund mustered forces numerous times throughout the country in 1016, beating Canute repeatedly and doggedly pursuing him to the eastern coast. Eadric (and presumably many other fickle lords) then switched their allegiance back to Edmund. Finally, the *Chronicle* records that Canute made a last stand against the English at "a hill called Ashingdon."[102] There, Eadric undermined the king's cause by fleeing from battle, leaving the remaining forces to suffer a catastrophic defeat at the hands of Canute. Some of the figures discussed in previous chapters fought and died in this battle. Ælfric of Hampshire (the treacherous ealdorman who had deserted in 992 and feigned illness in 1003) died honorably while fighting for King Edmund. So too did Ulfcytel, known for his famed stand against the Vikings in 1004.

After this, Canute and Edmund reached a formal agreement to divide the kingdom — Edmund would rule Wessex, while Canute would control Mercia and the north. But Edmund's own death in November 1016 allowed Canute to take the rest of the kingdom without a fight, ending Saxon control over England for a generation.

While Edmund's early success against Canute is often held up in contrast to Æthelred's military career, it is worth noting that Canute suffered severe defeats at the hands of both father and son. In 1014, Æthelred had expelled Canute from the country entirely, something that Edmund would never accomplish. While Canute would go on to rule a vast North Sea Empire and become a genuinely effective "English" king, his start was rough. It seems that, in regard to their reputations, Æthelred and Canute both suffer from a form of confirmation bias. Because Æthelred is seen as an overall bad king, his victories in 1014 are chalked up to good luck or omitted entirely. Canute's constant military breakdowns from 1014-16, on the other hand, are typically downplayed or excused because Canute would go on to be seen as a strong king.

In reality, the political and military situation in England from 1014-16 was far more complex.[103] For example, take this scenario: a legitimate king of England finds his borders invaded by a commander from overseas. This commander first occupies the land, then attacks the king, and finally forces the king to flee his country. In this exercise, Æthelred, Sweyn, and Canute can be variously substituted into these roles and the scenario still holds true historically: in 1013, Æthelred was forced out by Sweyn, who then became the legitimate ruler of England as "full king." In 1014, Æthelred was the invader who forced the next legitimate king, Canute, out of the country.

It is understandable that shorter works, such as encyclopedia entries or general overviews of the Viking Age, do not recognize these nuances. They only have so much space to devote to these years, and sometimes the only way to make sense of complex events in a short space is to simplify them — the bad king Æthelred suffers a gradual, linear decline while Canute experiences a contrasting rise to power. However, the war surrounding the Danish Conquest was anything but linear. One side would gain the upper hand, only to lose it dramatically and then recover. Canute conquered England in 1016, but the outcome could easily have been different. The war between the English and the Danes was a far closer contest than is commonly recognized, with plenty of turns, bumps, and surprises.

Many of the figures who interacted with Æthelred continued to influence English politics for decades after his death. His widow, Emma, married Canute and retained her power in England. She holds the distinction of being married to two kings and being the mother of two more — one from each husband.[104] Canute would go on to reign for nearly 20 years, dying suddenly in 1035. Others, like Eadric, were not so lucky. Canute had him executed in 1017. Still others returned to the history books in the most roundabout ways. Young Edward, who had delivered Æthelred's message of forgiveness during the restoration agreement of 1014, is one such example. After spending over 25 years in exile, Edward was, amazingly, the last man standing in the line of succession in 1042, becoming King of England and restoring Æthelred's bloodline to power. Today he is known as St. Edward the Confessor, and his death set up the more-famous events of 1066.

Returning to Æthelred, it is clear that reputations are not always what they seem. As the redeemed Ælfric of Hampshire showed us, legacies are complicated. While it would be overreacting to place Æthelred in the company of full-blown warrior kings like Edward III and William the Conqueror, he was neither a military failure nor by any means a battle-avoider. Æthelred's long reign reveals a monarch who, even if ultimately unsuccessful, was far from militarily inactive. The king ordered and participated in over a dozen major campaigns: he built fleets, organized armies, led his men into battle, defended his cities, and retaliated against his enemies. Some of these endeavors were failures, like the fleets of 992 and 1009, or his invasion of Normandy around 1000. Some were inconsequential successes, like the razing of Rochester in 986 or the destruction of Strathclyde and the Isle of Man in 1000. However, Æthelred also led resounding triumphs, such as his re-conquest of 1014.

The final verdict on Æthelred's military abilities, while they will never be viewed as exceptional, should be far more measured. The king faced an extremely difficult enemy, yet he experienced more military success than normally given credit for. Rather than being viewed as a reluctant or failed commander, Æthelred should be seen for what he was — a survivor and a fighter.

BIBLIOGRAPHY

Abels, Richard. *Æthelred the Unready: The Failed King*. London: Penguin, 2018.

"Æthelred II restores to the see of Rochester six sulungs at Bromley and the use of forest in the Weald. A.D. 998." In the *Textus Roffensis*. Translated by Christopher Monk. *Rochester Cathedral Research Guild*, 2017.

Andersson, Theodore M. "The Viking Policy of Ethelred the Unready." *Scandinavian Studies* 59, no. 3 (Summer 1987): 284-295. https://www.jstor.org/stable/40918864.

The Anglo-Saxon Chronicle. Translated by George Norman Garmonsway. London: J.M. Dent & Sons, 1954. Reprint, 1990.

Barlow, Frank. *Edward the Confessor*. University of California Press, 1970. Reprint, New Haven: Yale University Press, 2011.

"The Battle of Maldon." In *The Norton Anthology of English Literature Online*. Translated by E.T. Donaldson. https://www.wwnorton.com/college/english/nael/n oa/pdf/01Maldon_1_6.pdf.

Bracewell, Patricia. "The Death of King Æthelred." Posted April 22, 2018. www.patriciabracewell. com/2018/04/the-death-of- aethelred/.

Braekman, W. "Wyrdwriteras: an Unpublished Ælfrician Text in Manuscript Hatton 115." *Revue belge de Philologie et d'Histoire* 44, no. 3 (1966): 959-970.

Edmonds, Fiona. "The expansion of the kingdom of Strathclyde." *Early Medieval Europe* 23, no. 1 (2015): 43-66. https://doi.org/10.1111/emed.12087.

Edmonds, Fiona. "The emergence and transformation of medieval Cumbria." *Scottish Historical Review* 93, no. 2 (October 2014): 195-216. https://doi.org/10.3366/shr.2014.0216.

Ferguson, Robert. *The Vikings*. London: Penguin, 2009.

Hagland, Jan Ragnar and Bruce Watson. "Fact or Folklore? The Viking attack on London Bridge." *London Archaeology* 10, no. 12 (Spring 2005). http://archaeologydataservice.ac.uk/archiveDS/archiveDownload?t=arch-457-1/dissemination/pdf/vol10/vol10_12/10_12_328_3 33.pdf.

Howard, Ian. *Sweyn Forkbeard's Invasions and the Danish Conquest of England, 991-1017*. Suffolk: Boydell & Brewer, 2003.

Keynes, Simon. "A Tale of Two Kings. Alfred the Great and Æthelred the Unready." *Transactions of the Royal Historical Society* 36 (1986): 195-217. https://doi.org/10.2307/3679065.

Keynes, Simon. "An abbot, an archbishop, and the viking raids of 1006-7 and 1009-12." *Anglo-Saxon England* 36 (Dec 2007): 151-220. https://www.jstor.org/stable/44510965.

Lacey, Robert, and Danny Danziger. *The Year 1000: What Life was like at the Turn of the First Millennium*. Little, Brown and Company, 1998.

Lavelle, Ryan. *Aethelred II: King of the English 978-1016.* Stroud: Tempus, 2002.

Meehan, Bernard. "The Siege of Durham, the Battle of Carham and the Cession of Lothian." *The Scottish Historical Review* 55, no. 1 (April 1976): 1-19. https://www.jstor.org/stable/25529143.

Morris, Christopher J. *Marriage and Murder in eleventh-century Northumbria: a study of 'De Obsessione Dunelmi.'* York: Borthwick Institute of Historical Research, University of York, 1992.

Osbern of Canterbury, *Vita S. Dunstani.* Translated by William Stubbs, 117.

Parker, Eleanor. *Dragon Lords: The History and Legends of Viking England.* I.B. Tauris, 2018.

Parker, Eleanor. *A Short History of the Danish Conquest.* Rounded Globe, 2016. https://roundedglobe. com/books/f067b2a6-0eb3-4479-8307- 2b242adcc3aa/A%20Short%20History%20of%20 the%20Danish%20Conquest/.

Ribman, Ronald. *The Ceremony of Innocence.* Broadway Theatre Archive, 1970.

Roach, Levi. *Æthelred The Unready.* New Haven: Yale University Press, 2016.

Scholz, Bernard W. "Sulcard of Westminster: 'Prologus de Construccione Westmonasterri.'" *Traditio* 20, (1964): 59-91.

Sheppard, Alice. *Families of the King: Writing Identity in the Anglo-Saxon Chronicle.* Toronto: University of Toronto Press, 2004.

Snorri Sturluson, *The Saga of Olafr Haraldsson (The Saint).* Translated by Alison Finlay and Anthony Faulkes.

London: Viking Society for Northern Studies, University College London, 2014.

Starkey, David. "Ængla-Land." *Monarchy with David Starkey*. Channel 4, 2004.

Stenton, Frank. *Anglo-Saxon England*, 8th ed. Oxford: Oxford University Press, 2001.

"Viking mass grave linked to elite killers of the medieval world." *University of Cambridge Research*, January 25, 2012. http://www.cam.ac.uk/research/news/viking-mass-grave-linked-to-elite-killers-of-the-medieval-world.

Wilcox, Jonathan. "The St. Brice's Day Massacre and Archbishop Wulfstan." *Peace and Negotiation: Strategies for Coexistence in the Middle Ages and the Renaissance*, edited by Diane Wolfthal, 79-91. Turnhout: Brepols, 2000. Quoted in *Classical and Medieval Literature Criticism* 59. Edited by Lynn M. Zott. Detroit: Gale, 2003. *Literature Resource Center*.

William of Jumieges. *Gesta Normannorum Ducum*. Translated by Elisabeth M. C. Van Houts. Oxford: Clarendon Press, 1995.

William of Malmesbury. "The History of the Kings of England." In *The Church Historians of England Vol III Part I*. Translated Joseph Stevenson. London: Seeley's, 1854.

Williams, Ann. *Æthelred the Unready: The Ill-Counseled King*. Bloomsbury Academic, 2003.

Williams, Ann. "Princeps Merciorum gentis: the family, career and connections of Ælfhere, ealdorman of Mercia, 956-83." *Anglo-Saxon England* 10 (1982): 143-72.

Williams, T. J. "Landscape and warfare in Anglo-Saxon England and the Viking campaign of 1006." *Early Medieval Europe* 23, no. 3 (August 2015). http://doi.org/10.1111/emed.12107.

Wood, Michael. "In Search of Ethelred the Unready." *In Search of the Dark Ages*. BBC, 1981.

NOTES

1. While the English referred to all Scandinavian raiders as Danes, I have chosen to use the more general term "Viking" since many "Danes" were actually Norwegian or Swedish. I will use Dane to refer specifically to people from Denmark.

2. *The Anglo-Saxon Chronicle*, trans. G.N. Garmonsway (London: J.M. Dent & Sons, 1954. Reprint: 1990), hereafter abbreviated in the footnotes as *ASC*.

3. William of Malmesbury, "The History of the Kings of England," in *The Church Historians of England Vol III Part I*, trans. Joseph Stevenson (London: Seeley's, 1854), 148.

4. Ronald Ribman, *The Ceremony of Innocence* (Broadway Theatre Archive, 1970).

5. Robert Ferguson, *The Vikings* (London: Penguin, 2009), 327.

6. Frank Barlow, *Edward the Confessor* (University of California Press, 1970. Reprint, New Haven: Yale University Press, 2011), 4.

7.   Michael Wood, "In Search of Ethelred the Unready," *In Search of the Dark Ages* (BBC, 1981).

8.   Ryan Lavelle, *Aethelred II: King of the English 978-1016* (Stroud: Tempus, 2002); Ann Williams, *Æthelred the Unready: The Ill-Counseled King* (Bloomsbury Academic, 2003); Levi Roach, *Æthelred The Unready* (New Haven: Yale University Press, 2016); Richard Abels, *Æthelred the Unready: The Failed King* (London: Penguin, 2018).

9.   Ian Howard, *Sweyn Forkbeard's Invasions and the Danish Conquest of England, 991-1017*, (Suffolk: Boydell & Brewer, 2003).

10. Æthelred's exact date of birth is unknown, but he is generally thought to have been born between 966-68, based on when he enters recorded history.

11. *ASC*. Eadred fought against Eric in 948. Eric returned to Northumbria before being displaced again in 954.

12. *Pacificus*. Alternate translations like "Peacemaker" and "Peaceable" are also common.

13. Æthelred and Edward had different mothers. Æthelred's mother held the title of queen and Edward's did not.

14. "Pirate hosts from the north" raided southern England between 980 and 982, but the *Chronicle* makes no mention of further attacks from 983-86.

15. Alice Sheppard, *Families of the King: Writing Identity in the Anglo-Saxon Chronicle* (Toronto: University of Toronto Press, 2004), 86. Sheppard also points out that the *Chronicle* does not provide us with any of the complicated political context surrounding the Rochester incident.

16. "Æthelred II restores to the see of Rochester six sulungs at Bromley and the use of forest in the Weald. A.D. 998" in the *Textus Roffensis*, trans. Christopher Monk, *Rochester Cathedral Research Guild*, 2017.

17. Bernard W. Scholz, "Sulcard of Westminster: 'Prologus de Construccione Westmonasterri,'' *Traditio* 20 (1964): 59- 91, http://www.jstor.org/stable/27830769.

18. Osbern of Canterbury, *Vita S. Dunstani*, trans. William Stubbs, 117.

19. Scott Thompson Smith, "The Edgar Poems and the poetics of failure in the Anglo-Saxon Chronicle," *Anglo- Saxon England* 39 (2011): 107-137. Smith analyzes the Chronicle's view of Edgar as a holy king and a friend to Benedictine reformers, while contrasting this sentiment with the loss of favor the reformers suffered in the reigns of Edward and Æthelred.

20. Ann Williams, "Princeps Merciorum gentis: the family, career and connections of Ælfhere, ealdorman of Mercia, 956-83," *Anglo-Saxon England* 10 (1982): 166.

21. A. Williams, *Æthelred the Unready*, 27.

22. For the poem itself, see "The Battle of Maldon," in *The Norton Anthology of English Literature Online*, trans. E.T. Donaldson, https://www.wwnorton.com/college/english/nael/noa/p df/01Maldon_1_6.pdf.

23. An ealdorman was a regional or territorial leader in late Anglo-Saxon England. In theory, they were appointed by the king, but in practice the office could become hereditary and was roughly analogous to the later term earl.

24. *ASC.*

25. *ASC.*

26. "Levies" refer to the English armies in the *Chronicle*. "To raise levies" means to call upon the available fighting men in an area and amass them into an army.

27. *ASC.*

28. *ASC.*

29. Roach, 107. Although the charter Roach refers to "is suspect," he argues strongly in favor of Ælfgar appropriating lands from the church.

30. *ASC.*

31. Theodore M. Andersson, "The Viking Policy of Ethelred the Unready," *Scandinavian Studies* 59, no. 3 (Summer 1987), https://www.jstor.org/stable/40918864.

32. *ASC*.

33. *ASC*.

34. Howard likewise interprets the attacks of 997-98 as "temporary, local difficulties," 52.

35. Roach, 179.

36. Robert Lacey and Danny Danziger, *The Year 1000: What Life was like at the Turn of the First Millennium*, (Little, Brown and Company, 1998), 67.

37. Howard, 53.

38. Abels, 79-80.

39. Lacey and Danziger, 67.

40. Roach, 180.

41. Lavelle, 97.

42. Wood.

43. Fiona Edmonds, "The expansion of the kingdom of Strathclyde," *Early Medieval Europe* 23, no. 1 (2015): 64-66, https://doi.org/10.1111/emed.12087.

44. Frank Stenton, *Anglo-Saxon England*, 8th ed. (Oxford: Oxford University Press, 2001): 379.

45. Sheppard, 87.

46. Fiona Edmonds, "The emergence and transformation of medieval Cumbria," *Scottish Historical Review* 93, no. 2 (October 2014): 208, https://doi.org/10.3366/shr.2014.0216. Brackets mine.

47. *ASC.*

48. *ASC.*

49. Lavelle, 97. The charter is from 1001.

50. Howard, 53.

51. Exact date unclear. Lavelle (97-99) places the battle in 1000, while Roach (187) places it in 1002.

52. Roach, 117.

53. William of Jumieges, *Gesta Normannorum Ducum*, trans. Elisabeth M. C. Van Houts (Clarendon Press, 1995).

54. Despite William of Jumieges' inclusion of these colorful details, experts like Lavelle (99) readily accept the account's overall premise; others, like Roach (187), are more cautious.

55. *ASC.*

56. *ASC*; an entry for 1011 complains that the king did not offer tribute "in time, but when they had done their worst."

57. A. Williams, *Æthelred the Unready*, 52-53.

58. Simon Keynes, "A Tale of Two Kings: Alfred the Great and *Æthelred the Unready*," *Transactions of the Royal Historical Society* 36 (1986): 211, https://doi.org/10.2307/3679065.

59. "Viking mass grave linked to elite killers of the medieval world," *University of Cambridge Research*, January 25, 2012, http://www.cam.ac.uk/research/news/viking-mass-grave- linked-to-elite-killers-of-the-medieval-world.

60. For more on St. Brice's Day, see Jonathan Wilcox, "The St. Brice's Day Massacre and Archbishop Wulfstan," in *Peace and Negotiation: Strategies for Coexistence in the Middle Ages and the Renaissance*, edited by Diane Wolfthal, 79-91 (Turnhout: Brepols, 2000). Quoted in *Classical and Medieval Literature Criticism* 59, edited by Lynn M. Zott (Detroit: Gale, 2003), *Literature Resource Center*.

61. Roach, 192.

62. For a translation of *De obsessione Dunelmi*, see Christopher J. Morris, *Marriage and Murder in eleventh-century Northumbria: a study of 'De Obsessione Dunelmi'* (York: Borthwick Institute of Historical Research, University of York, 1992), 1-5; for more on *De obsessione* and its connection to the *Annals of Ulster*, see Bernard Meehan, "The Siege of Durham, the Battle of Carham and the Cession of Lothian," *The Scottish Historical Review* 55, no. 1 (April 1976): 4, https://www.jstor.org/stable/25529143.

63. Lavelle 106-08, A. Williams, *Æthelred the Unready*, 71-75.

64. Lavalle, 108.

65. Lavalle also summarizes Keynes' view on p. 108.

66. For more on the local response in 1006, see T. J. Williams, "Landscape and warfare in Anglo-Saxon England and the Viking campaign of 1006," *Early Medieval Europe* 23, no. 3 (August 2015).

67. W. Braekman, "Wyrdwriteras: an Unpublished Ælfrician Text in Manuscript Hatton 115," *Revue belge de Philologie et d'Histoire* 44, no. 3 (1966): 963-64, http://www.persee.fr/doc/rbph_0035-0818_1966_num_44_3_2642; Simon Keynes, "An abbot, an archbishop, and the viking raids of 1006-7 and 1009-12," *Anglo-Saxon England* 36 (Dec 2007): 165, https://www.jstor.org/stable/44510965.

68. *ASC*.

69. The *Chronicle* says that Wulfnoth fled because Ealdorman Eadric's brother, Beorhtric, "made accusations" against him. Exactly what Wulfnoth was accused of is unknown.

70. Abels, 70.

71. *ASC*.

72. Snorri Sturluson, *The Saga of Olafr Haraldsson (The Saint)*, trans. Alison Finlay and Anthony Faulkes (London: Viking Society for Northern Studies, University College London, 2014).

73. *ASC*.

74. *ASC*.

75. *ASC*.

76. *ASC*.

77. *ASC*.

78. *ASC*.

79. William of Malmesbury's statement (p. 48 of Stevenson's *Church Historians*) is notable since he is otherwise highly critical of Æthelred.

80. *ASC.*

81. Lady Jane Grey technically ruled for nine days in July 1553, but her status as monarch remains disputed. Traditionally, the start of Sweyn's reign is placed around Christmas 1013, once Æthelred had left the country.

82. *ASC*; "rightful lord" is sometimes translated as "natural lord."

83. The *Chronicle* does not say that Æthelstan and Edmund fled with Emma, Æthelred, or their young sons.

84. In the 9th century, Æthelbald seized control of Wessex and forced his father, Æthelwulf, to abdicate; they ended up splitting the kingdom between them, with Æthelbald controlling Wessex and his father restricted to eastern parts of the kingdom. From 957-59, the kingdom was split again between Eadwig in the south and Edgar in the north.

85. *ASC.*

86. I have borrowed the phrase "Anglo-Saxon Magna Carta" from David Starkey's "Ængla-Land," *Monarchy with David Starkey* (Channel 4, 2004).

87. *ASC.*

88. Snorri Sturluson.

89. Canute himself may not have been present if Snorri's account is to be trusted. Canute would have been farther north in Lindsey at this time.

90. Jan Ragnar Hagland and Bruce Watson, "Fact or Folklore? The Viking attack on London Bridge," *London Archaeology* 10, no. 12 (Spring 2005), http://archaeologydataservice.ac.uk/archiveDS/ archiveDownload?t=arch-457-1/dissemination/pdf/ vol10/vol10_12/10_12_328_333.pdf.

91. For more on the legend of St. Edmund and Sweyn, see Eleanor Parker, *Dragon Lords: The History and Legends of Viking England* (I.B. Tauris, 2018), 44-47. Parker traces the earliest versions of this saintly encounter back to the 1090s, long before the *Saga* was written.

92. The five kings preceding Æthelred had all died by their early 30s.

93. Wood.

94. *ASC.*

95. *ASC.*

96. Probably the Five Boroughs and the Danelaw.

97. Patricia Bracewell, "The Death of King Æthelred," posted April 22, 2018, www.patriciabracewell.com/2018/04/ the-death-of-aethelred/.

98. *ASC*.

99. "King Edmund Ætheling." Ætheling was a designation reserved for men of royal blood (often rendered "Prince"), although it is unusual to see it paired with "King." The awkward phrasing may suggest that it comes from a period in 1015 or 1016 when Edmund was still at odds with his father. However, it may date from just after Æthelred's death and merely represent Edmund emphasizing his English royal blood (as opposed to his Danish rival).

100. Lavelle, 134. In the chronicler's defense, Æthelred had been betrayed by Ælfric in 992, Pallig in 1001, Wulfnoth Cild in 1009, Edmund in 1015, Eadric in 1016, and possibly Thorkell in 1016, as well.

101. Keynes, "A Tale of Two Kings," 216. Keynes likewise infers that this illness killed Æthelred.

102. *ASC*.

103. For more on the Danish Conquest, see Eleanor Parker, *A Short History of the Danish Conquest* (Rounded Globe, 2016), https://roundedglobe.com/books/ f067b2a6-0eb3-4479-8307-2b242adcc3aa/A%20 Short%20History%20of%20the%20 Danish%20 Conquest/.

104. Harthacanute, Emma's son by Canute, ruled England from 1040-42 and claimed the throne from 1035-40. Edward, her son by Æthelred, would rule from 1042-1066

GLOSSARY

Ætheling – a male member of the royal family, close in meaning to "prince"

Anglo-Saxon England – a term broadly used for the period spanning from the Anglo-Saxon migration from Germany, in the 5th century, to the Norman Conquest of 1066. More narrowly, it also can refer to the Kingdom of England from its unification under Æthelstan until the Norman Conquest. Residents of Anglo-Saxon England are frequently referred to, often interchangeably, as Anglo-Saxon, English, or Saxon

Burh – a fortified town or city

Danelaw – areas in eastern and northern England where the laws and customs of the Danes were followed. In Æthelred's time, this area was under English authority but was still heavily populated by Scandinavians and Viking descendants

Ealdorman – a regional or territorial governor, roughly analogous to "earl"

King of the English – the title used for English rulers in the 10th and early 11th centuries; earlier kings had used phrasing like "King of the Anglo-Saxons," while the more-familiar "King of England" title was not used until after Æthelred's time

Levies – available fighting men, armies; used to refer specifically to English forces in the *Chronicle*

Reeve – a local official; origin of the modern word sheriff ("shire reeve")

Tribute – payment made to an invading force, usually in exchange for peace

Witan – a loosely-defined group of royal advisors and councilors; the witan had no formal membership or permanent meeting place, but usually included the prominent nobles and churchmen in a given region

INDEX

ABOUT THE AUTHOR

Brandon M. Bender is a writer from Kansas City whose work covers a wide range of topics. He made his publication debut at 19, contributing a series of articles to *The Kansas City Star* (2013-14). Since then, he has won several local and regional awards for his work on medieval history (*The Kansas Association of Historians*, 2018), American history (*Hare & Bell*, 2018), short fiction (*The League for Innovation*, 2016; *Kansas Voices*, 2019), and poetry (*Mind's Eye*, 2018). Bender's publications can also be found in *365 Days*, *Scholar Space*, and others.

Bender works full-time supervising a team of proofreaders in the corporate world and has also worked as a content editor for the *Blue Monday Review* literary magazine. You can follow him at <u>brandonmichaelbender.com</u>.

Printed in Great Britain
by Amazon

65274429R00061